Eminent Maricones

LIVING OUT
Gay and Lesbian Autobiographies

Joan Larkin and David Bergman
GENERAL EDITORS

Midlife Queer: Autobiography of a Decade, 1971–1981
Martin Duberman

Widescreen Dreams: Growing Up Gay at the Movies
Patrick E. Horrigan

Eminent Maricones: Arenas, Lorca, Puig, and Me
Jaime Manrique

Taboo
Boyer Rickel

Eminent Maricones

ARENAS, LORCA, PUIG,
AND ME

Jaime Manrique

The University of Wisconsin Press

The University of Wisconsin Press
1930 Monroe Street, 3rd Floor
Madison, Wisconsin 53711-2059
uwpress.wisc.edu

3 Henrietta Street
London WC2E 8LU, England
eurospanbookstore.com

Printed in the United States of America

Library of Congress Cataloging-in-Publication Data
Manrique, Jaime, 1949–
Eminent maricones : Arenas, Lorca, Puig, and me / Jaime Manrique.
126 pp. cm. — (Living out : gay and lesbian autobiographies)
ISBN 0-299-16180-3 (cloth : alk. paper)
1. Manrique, Jaime, 1949– . 2. Authors, Colombian—20th
century—Biography. 3. Authors, Spanish American—20th century—
Biography. 4. Authors, Spanish—20th century—Biography. 5. Gay
men—Latin America—Biography. 6. Gay men—Spain—Biography.
I. Title. II. Series: Living out.
PQ8180.23.A52Z74 1999
868—dc21
[b]   98-49022

ISBN 978-0-299-16184-2 (pbk.: alk. paper)
ISBN 978-0-299-16183-5 (e-book)

This book couldn't be for anyone else but Manuel and Reinaldo

Contents

Acknowledgments   ix

1. Legs: A Memoir of Childhood and Adolescence   3
2. Manuel Puig: The Writer as Diva   39
3. The Last Days of Reinaldo Arenas: A Sadness
   as Deep as the Sea   62
4. Federico García Lorca and Internalized Homophobia   70
5. The Other Jaime Manrique: A Dead Soul   103
6. Nowadays   112

Source Information   115

Acknowledgments

"Manuel Puig: The Writer as Diva" appeared in English in *Christopher Street* (July 1993) and in Spanish in *Exceso* (Caracas, 1993) and *Página 16* (Buenos Aires, 1994). "The Last Days of Reinaldo Arenas: A Sadness as Deep as the Sea" was published in the *Washington Post Book World* (November 7, 1993). A shorter version first appeared in English in the *PEN American Center Newsletter* (1991) and in Spanish in *Exceso* (1991). A shorter version of "Federico García Lorca and Internalized Homophobia" was published as "Federico García Lorca: Eminent Maricón" in *Hopscotch* (1998). "The Other Jaime Manrique: A Dead Soul," appeared in *The World 55* (1999).

I would like to thank Dionisio Cañas for making important information about Lorca's relationship with Philip Cummings available to me; Tom Colchie for introducing me to Reinaldo Arenas; and Bill Sullivan for the times he shared with Manuel, Reinaldo, and me.

But my deepest thanks are for Pauline Kael, whose voice made me fall in love with English prose and whose generous suggestions were invaluable help in shaping a few sections of this book.

Eminent Maricones

1

Legs
A Memoir of Childhood
and Adolescence

This is my first memory: I'm taking a shower with one of my young aunts and I'm reaching for her pubis. She giggles and swirls around me. I'm standing on my own, but I don't talk yet. The bathroom where we're showering is the only place in our house I vaguely remember. The white-washed walls are damp, streaked with lichen growing around the edges of the cement floor. The house is in the town of Ciénaga, which means swamp. I know we lived in that house for the first two years of my life because of surviving telegrams sent to our house on Nuevo Callejón for my first two birthdays.

Before I was born, my parents kept a house on the outskirts of the Colombian village of Río Frío, on one of my father's banana plantations.

I don't know how my parents met. Because of a surviving telegram to my mother in Barranquilla, dated November 15, 1944, I know that Soledad Ardila and Gustavo Manrique met sometime toward the end of 1944: "Received your telegram. Without you I can't live. Let me know when you're ready to return. Kisses. Gustavo." And, in a letter to my mother of October 11, 1945, my father writes: "You don't know how much I'm thinking of you as we approach the anniversary of the day on which I was so fortunate to meet you."

It seems that my parents met in Barranquilla, where my mother had gone "to sew" (my grandmother told me this when I was forty). My father was a married man and lived with his wife and children in the Caribbean port of Santa Marta. My mother's story is shrouded in mystery. Apparently, she was married to a man by the name of Leal. I conclude this because of a number of telegrams my father sent to my mother when she visited her father's home in El Banco in 1945. The telegrams are addressed to Soledad

3

Ardila de Leal. I remember too seeing, among my mother's papers during my childhood and adolescence, a picture of a little boy in his coffin. This child, it seems, was conceived in that marriage.

Just about everything I know about my parents before I was born I've learned from fifty-six telegrams and thirty-six letters my father sent to my mother from November 15, 1944, to November 16, 1951, and from *The Story of Our Baby* (my baby book), in which many of the main events of the first six years of my life were recorded. In my childhood my mother would often remind my sister and me that these letters represented proof that we were our father's children—because he refused to acknowledge us legally as his offspring. I grew up thinking of these letters as a weapon, precious documents that would eventually entitle me to my rightful share of my father's estate. The letters proved unnecessary in that regard, because my father (as he had always promised) acknowledged us as his children in his last will and testament.

I was at my mother's house for Christmas 1989, rummaging through my bedroom closet one night, when my father's correspondence to my mother, along with my baby book, fell into my hands. I couldn't quite believe my eyes: that spring a fire had raged throughout my mother's house, destroying most of my books and almost all my early manuscripts and correspondence. And yet these documents had survived untouched. That night I read the letters for the first time in many years, and they unsettled me in a way I could not have foreseen. Reading the letters, I heard my father's voice as he was at the time he wrote them—a man in his midforties, a man deeply in love. Because I had hardly known my father, the letters revealed him to me in a surprising way: they were so passionate and eloquent that I realized I was a writer because of him.

To me, these extant documents were an omen. My mother had saved them for almost five decades; they had traveled from Colombia to the States; they had survived a fire. Now I understood that she treasured them as much for being proof of her children's legitimacy as for their being great love letters to her. My father's passion for my mother was so searing that I was overcome with sensual languor just reading these documents. I was almost as old as my father was when he wrote them, and these letters made me sad. I had never loved anyone so intensely, nor had anyone loved me with such an ardent display of passion and for such a long period of time. I felt as though the man who had written them half a century ago was more alive than I felt reading them.

My father was born in Ibagué, a small Andean town in the interior of Colombia, on November 15, 1901. My paternal grandparents were

Antonio Manrique Arango and María Eusebia Alvarez Uribe. In Colombian society those names are as blue chip as you can get. I've been told by my mother that my paternal grandfather was a general in the Colombian army. My father enlisted and served on the island of San Andrés in the Caribbean, where he attained the rank of sergeant. I've seen a couple of pictures of my father around this time looking dapper in a white suit and straw hat. He's movie-star handsome, slender, manly, a beautifully bred stud—the picture of a winner.

My father was in his midtwenties when he moved to the mainland, specifically, the Atlantic coast of Colombia. Here he must have met Josefina Danies Bermudes, an heiress and member of one of the most prominent families in Santa Marta, the oldest Spanish city in South America. They were married on April 21, 1932.

Besides his good looks, my father's main asset was his ancient and distinguished name, which goes all the way back to the time of the Holy Roman Empire. The first famous Manriques appear in Spain in the fifteenth century. They are poets as well as warriors. Jorge Manrique, one of the most influential poets in Spanish literature, wrote *Couplets on the Death of My Father* circa 1476. Manrique, a captain, died in 1479 of wounds sustained in battle and was survived by his wife and several children, one of them male. The last historical reference to this male heir is in 1515, and he apparently died without children. However, Jorge Manrique was one of many children. His father, Don Rodrigo, the famous warrior who in 1474 won military jurisdiction over Castile, freeing it from the Moors, had married three times. The vicereine of New Spain, María Luisa Manrique de Lara y Gonzaga (patron of the Mexican nun Sor Juana Inés de La Cruz), and Viceroy Alvaro Manrique y Zuñiga, seventh viceroy of New Spain, were descended from these Manriques. The viceroy arrived in the New World in 1585. He was an eccentric man who traveled with his coffin, in which he slept. My father's family descends from these Manriques. Several Manriques of note lived during Colombia's colonial period—their portraits hang in many libraries and museums of Bogotá. In the nineteenth century, the Manrique family in Colombia produced a few writers and journalists.

This is one of the few memories I have of my father in my childhood: I am in my parents' bedroom; my father is in bed, wearing aquamarine cotton pajamas. I am holding my nanny's hand and my father asks me to repeat after him: "I am Jaime Manrique Ardila Alvarez Arango Uribe Benítez Salázar Santamaría, a blue blood!"

My maternal grandparents—the Ardilas—were peasants of mixed white, Indian, and African blood. My grandfather, José Ardila Puerta, and my grandmother, Serafina Ardila, were first cousins. José Ardila Puerta, my grandfather, told me his story one December afternoon in 1972 when we were visiting Barranco de Loba, the river hamlet where my grandparents were born. He was an only child who grew up with his mother (he did not mention his father). They were poor. Still in his teens, my grandfather decided to emigrate to Cuba to make his fortune. He journeyed down river to the port of Barranquilla, then a departure point for Havana. To earn money for his passage, my grandfather built a raft and cut wood in the swamps surrounding the city. Eventually, he bought a ticket, but the night before he was to leave he got drunk and missed his boat.

My grandfather decided to return home. Again he earned money chopping wood and used his savings to buy goods to barter in the towns and settlements along the banks of the Magdalena River. Buying and reselling, he eventually made his way back up river to Barranco de Loba. The trip was a success after all: he didn't make it to Cuba, but he made enough money to buy his first cow and his first plot of land, La Esperanza. He became affluent.

Now a man of means, he started his first family with Serafina Ardila, my grandmother. They didn't get married because she was not his equal. Whereas he had "traveled," could read and write, and was *moreno* (a light-skinned black), my grandmother was illiterate and of pure African descent. Their first child was my mother, Soledad, born in 1919. My uncle José Antonio was born in 1922.

Several years later, my grandfather began his second family with Berta Feria. She was light-skinned enough to pass for white, and she had attended convent school.

My grandmother Serafina (Mamá Fina) is still alive and is almost a hundred years old. After my grandfather deserted her, she bore children by several men. Her children are my aunts and uncles, but because they are poor, uneducated, and black, and because Colombia is a racist and classist society, when I was growing up I wasn't encouraged to acknowledge them as my relatives. In fact, I was ashamed of them.

With my step-grandmother, Papá José had ten children. All went to school, some graduated from college, and a few have been successful in the world. They were the uncles and aunts my mother encouraged me to acknowledge; they were the only family I ever knew. Until a few days before he died, my grandfather remained a Mason and rejected Catholicism.

My grandfather and my father were the same age. At my birth they were in their late forties and they resembled each other: portly men who carried themselves with great dignity, almost majesty. My mother has a photograph of my grandfather as a young man in a suit and hat that bears a strong resemblance to a picture of my father dressed up as a dandy—the peasant impersonating the aristocrat.

This is my second memory: I set fire to an empty plot of land across from our house, and then I hid in our backyard, behind some yucca plants. At that time we were living in a house in El Porvenir, a fashionable upper-middle-class suburb of Barranquilla. I must have been about five years old.

My next memory is of being expelled from Colegio Americano. I am in the principal's office with my mother, a classmate, and his mother. The boy accuses me of asking him to show me his penis in the bathroom. I don't deny the accusation, although it's hard for me to believe that I've done anything wrong.

I was six when my parents separated. Between the time of my first memory (taking a shower with my aunt), and my second and third memories, I remember nothing. The lacunae of these years I've been able to fill sketchily from the entries in my baby book, which notes such incidents as my first smile (when I was four days old—it was for my father). It also notes that by two and a half months I would break out in laughter. I know when I was baptized, who attended the ceremony, what presents I received and from whom. A sarcastic person, a sort of evil fairy godmother, has added (with a different pen): "From the Duke of Kent, who attended the party, he received a golden *eslabón* [a word that means both gold chain and highly poisonous snake] and from Princess Margaret, a 35 carats diamond." I know too about the first time I went out of the house; who took me to church for the first time; and about a trip in May 1950 to Santa Marta. Anastasia, my mother's goddaughter, accompanied my mother and me. From Santa Marta we went to visit the banana plantation in Río Frío, where we spent fifteen days. I was bathed in the icy waters of the river and caught a bad cold, after which dark spots appeared on my body.

My history of asthma begins after this trip. It became so severe in my childhood that I had to spend long periods by the seashore.

My first Christmas is recorded in the baby book, as well as the many presents I received and how I looked in the different outfits that friends and relatives gave me. Then there are no more entries until I'm five. This is what my aunt Aura has written: "On his fifth birthday, there was no birthday celebration because he had just arrived in Ciénaga, Magdalena, and he didn't yet have any little friends."

I do remember, as I write this, a trip by boat to Ciénaga and how my dog, Bobby Capó, jumped into the river in the night and disappeared. I'm aware that perhaps the dog did not jump off the boat but was thrown into the dark waters.

There is an entry for my sixth year. I had a birthday party, an event I remember vaguely, and my baby book contains a photograph of me, looking unhappy and surrounded by a group of beautifully dressed children. I remember that I cried a lot. The last entry in my baby book is for my seventh birthday: "On June 16, 1956, he was seven years old. That day there was no party because his younger brother was ill."

It occurs to me that I don't remember the births of my sister or brother, that I have no memories of my sister (three years younger than I) until I was seven. As I'm writing this, another memory resurfaces. We were living in our house in El Porvenir. My mother is having an abortion at home: I remember torrents of blood, that the fetuses are twins or triplets, and that someone (a woman) remarks it is a good thing my mother has aborted because they are girls.

I was born in Barranquilla on June 16, 1949. The following day, my father wrote to my mother from Río Frío: "I salute you and hope you're doing well and are happy with our sprout. You can't imagine how happy the news makes me and I wish I could be with you as I write this, but unfortunately I'm prevented from joining you by the many great commitments that keep me away from being next to you as is my desire. . . . I despair of seeing you as soon as possible, but until Tuesday I won't be able to enjoy that pleasure. . . . Be patient and remember I'm telling you the truth and that I love you very much."

Then, just three months after my birth, on September 11, he complains in a letter about how much money she spends; he even threatens to leave her because he cannot afford to keep her. On October 12, as is the custom among middle-class Colombian families, ads were taken in two newspapers announcing that Jaime Manrique Ardila, son of Gustavo Manrique and his wife Soledad Ardila de Manrique, had been baptized in Barranquilla. From then on the tone of his correspondence changes. Whereas in most letters of the previous five years he had addressed her as "My darling little black one," in a letter written eight days after my christening he addresses her formally, "Dear Soledad: I hadn't written earlier because I haven't had a free minute. You have no idea of the great scandal in Santa Marta and Ciénaga because of the thoughtlessness of the items in La Prensa and in El Siglo." (The former was a Santa Marta newspaper and the latter the most important conservative newspaper published in Bogotá. My father was a lifelong member of the Conservative Party, and this is the newspaper that he and his friends read.)

He continues: "The effect has been worse than an atomic bomb—it has been that unpleasant for me these past few days. It is impossible to tell you in detail what happened. Today I was in town to pick up a shipment of lime that Quiñones sent me, and I found some furniture that arrived to be picked up by José Ardila [my grandfather's name as well as the name of three of my uncles]. You can't imagine how surprised I was when I was told by the real estate agents in Ciénaga that they would not rent me the house, for any amount of money, because they know it is not going to be occupied by my family. I think that it would be impossible for me at this moment to carry out this project. We have to let the hard feelings calm down. I don't know who was the imbecile who thought of publishing such an item, but there was no need for it. This happens to you for not consulting things with me. Tomorrow, from Río Frío, I'll write in greater details. My wish is that Jaime and all the others in the house are fine. In the meantime, I send you hugs and kisses."

The following days he writes, "Darling little black one: As I told you in the note I sent yesterday, I want to explain to you, as much as I'm able to, all the upsets and troubles brought about by the items in La Prensa and El Siglo. As soon as I reached the airport, I received news of what had happened in Santa Marta. That night, my wife came looking for me and, very politely, asked for an explanation. I told her I was truly sorry, and that it was neither your fault nor mine. But I couldn't make her understand this. I went to Santa Marta that night and there I found six letters from the Directors of the Banks and people I do business with. They all wanted to know if it was true that I had married in Barranquilla, and, if that was the case, they asked me to settle all my pending business with them right away. My wife's family made long faces at me, as if they wanted to eat me up; and in the streets, some friends asked whether it was true and others stopped saying hello to me. Everyone stared at me as if I were a weird animal. Three days later, I received letters from my relatives in Bogotá regarding this matter, and my children were appalled and very ashamed about the publication of these items. For me, these have been the worst days of my life. So much so that I wanted to go hide some place where I would never be heard of again. In Ciénaga, all the people who know me behaved in the same manner, and Toño Riascos, from whom I had rented the house and to whom I had paid the first month's rent, sent a letter returning the check for the amount I had paid him and said that there was no amount of money, or attenuating circumstances, under which he would rent me the house.

"Because of all these reasons, I think it would be convenient to let some time go by, and, until everything simmers down, we have to wait.

"I can't begin to comprehend why anyone would do such a thing to me, because I don't have any enemies. I mean, I do harm to no one. I don't believe, either, that this was your idea. I don't think you are that vain or clumsy; but at any rate, we have been the only victims. Let me know if you've found out anything about the inquiries you were going to make at La Prensa, because it would be worthwhile to unmask my enemies, or at least to know who they are.

"Due to everything that's happened, we have to take precautions for the future and not trust anyone. I don't want you to worry anymore because the thunderstorm seems to be abating. Also, don't think I blame you in any way or that I will change toward you. All we have to do is to be a little more intelligent so we can erase all these bad impressions."

In retrospect, it seems to me that my birth meant different things to my parents. To my mother it was legitimation: she was no longer just another mistress of the banana baron but the mother of a Manrique. To my father my birth seems to have meant the end of the carefree days of the great romance of his life.

My father's letters to my mother end in 1951, when we are in Medellín, where we had gone seeking a better climate for my chronic asthma. I can't help thinking that my father couldn't have been too pleased with a son who was an invalid and who, from early on, brought scandal upon his illustrious name.

The circumstances of my parents' separation are unclear to me. This much I know for sure: my father left my mother for an airline attendant who was thirty-two years his junior.

I don't remember the birth of my brother Antonio José. He was a swarthy, hairy baby born with a heart murmur. I nicknamed him Popeye because of his overdeveloped upper arms. I heard my father denied Antonio José was his child (I suspect my mother was unfaithful to my father with Antonio Serge, a man who several years later became her lover). I also heard that my little brother's heart murmur was caused by my father's advanced age. (My father was fifty-five when Antonio José was born.) It's likely I disliked Antonio José because I blamed him for my parents' separation.

I did not miss my father; he had seldom been around anyway. But the circumstances surrounding the separation were distressing. I overheard my mother tell a friend that my father's new mistress had threatened her at church, with a gun, when my mother was pregnant with Antonio José. This incident was mentioned as another potential cause of his heart murmur.

Seeing our home dismantled, and my mother's retainers disbanded, was alarming. I also understood I was no longer a rich boy. My father gave my mother the house we lived in, another house he had bought for my baby sister, and a banana plantation.

We moved out of our house in El Porvenir. My mother may have just wanted a change of scene, or she may have been advised to move by Señora

Petra, the fortune-teller who was my mother's adviser. Our new home was situated in the middle-class neighborhood of Bellavista. In that house my mother received Patiño, a boyfriend. That was where my voyeurism began: I'd watch my mother and Patiño make love, and I'd become eroticized.

I was enrolled at Colegio Hebreo Unión, a Jewish school that did not care that my parents were not married to each other. I learned Hebrew before I knew how to read in Spanish, and I became a consummate practitioner of Israeli dances. My first memories of happiness are linked to that school. Most students were the children of European Jews who had arrived in Barranquilla during World War II or shortly after it ended. My best friend was a Swedish boy named Stick Luster. He was ash blond, spindly. His family had moved to Barranquilla because his father was an engineer for the phone company.

Stick was my first love. We'd skip school and go into the thick bush behind his house to build traps for rabbits and birds. One day I went to visit him, and his mother came to the door and told me I couldn't see Stick anymore because I was a bad influence. My heart was broken for the first time.

My little brother died when he was six months old. My sister and I were visiting friends of my mother's one Saturday afternoon when he died. My aunt Aura came to fetch us. She took us out on the terrace and asked us to sit on the cool tiles of the floor. Then, very seriously, she told us our little brother had gone to heaven.

The other major event of that period was learning to read in Spanish. I remember the exact moment when it happened: I was riding the school bus at noon, and I was poring over the "Tarzan" comic strip in the Sunday newspaper. For a couple of years I'd had followed the adventures of Tarzan in the comic strip by interpreting the colorful tableaux. Suddenly, I understood the words. I sat there quietly, shaking, as if caught in a long tremor that shook the world, noiselessly, steadily. I couldn't turn to the boy sitting next to me to explain what was happening. It was as if I already understood that the deepest feelings we have are impossible to communicate and ultimately meaningless to others. I felt as Balboa must have felt when he first glimpsed the Pacific: an unknown vastness opened in front of my eyes, and I grasped that my life would be forever richer, that great treasures lay in front of me, that I would never be the same, that I had found for myself something that represented a new life that would be there for me as long as I lived.

The bus stopped. I bolted from it and ran into my house screaming, "I can read! I can read!" Up until that point I had relied on my aunt Aura to read to me and to entertain me by telling me the folk tales of the Atlantic coast of Colombia. No other happiness I've experienced since can quite compare with the exhilaration and joy I felt as I sat in that bus and finally could read in Spanish.

We moved to Bogotá in 1956. The dictator Gustavo Rojas Pinilla was about to be overthrown. Gabriel García Márquez has talked about how moving from the Atlantic coast, where he was born, to study in the village of Zipaquirá, high in the Andes in the savannah of Bogotá, was a move from a world of light to one of shadows.

Bogotá back then was still a small colonial city, not the amorphous metropolis it is today. It was all those things García Márquez hated: chilly, rainy, somber, inhabited by people dressed in heavy black coats who seemed to be in perpetual mourning. But the city's melancholy suited me: Bogotá's remoteness, its gray misty mornings, its dense evening fog, its pluvious climate, and, above all, its emerald cordilleras, which gleamed on the rare occasions the sun came out and the ivory sunlight of the high Andes hit them. For a morbid child like me, there was no better place to be. The city was mysterious, close to the heritage of its pre-Columbian past. I loved the weeping willows lining the boulevards, the sensual jewel-like orchids growing in the parks, the groves of silvery aromatic eucalyptus, and the tall pines where prismatic hummingbirds nested.

The three of us—my mother, sister, and I—took a room in Lafayette, a boardinghouse in downtown Bogotá. My uncle Chelo, an engineering student, lived there. He was involved in the student uprisings that led to the overthrow of the dictator. Lafayette was on Carrera Séptima, and from its second floor windows I saw the army firing at—and wounding—demonstrators. One afternoon my uncle had to hurriedly climb a high wall and jump down onto the patio of the church adjoining Lafayette to escape the police. One story affected me: spectators at a bullfight were massacred in the bullring because they had booed the dictator's daughter. The dictator ordered the doors of the bullring closed and kept people locked up for days. Many young people were shot in full view.

From Lafayette I have the first strong memories of my sister. One day—it was Good Friday—we were playing with other children. My sister put her head through a broken window, and a sliver of glass stuck under her chin. She bled profusely and was rushed to the hospital, where she received stitches. That day at mass the priest had said that everything we did wounded the flesh of Christ. When we walked, we were walking on the flesh of Christ, the rough soles of our shoes scrapping his living flesh. When we sat on a chair, we sat on his flesh; when we cut a piece of food, we were cutting the flesh of Christ.

A new dance—*el merecumbé*—was the rage. It was invented by Pacho Galán whose orchestra was staying at Lafayette. I became friends with their lead singer, a beautiful and glamorous young woman from the Atlantic coast.

My mother had a friend in Bogotá, Goyita, whose daughter, Fanny, was married to an older man who had a son, Guillermito, my age. We would visit them for elevenses, which consisted of hot chocolate, white cheese, stuffed figs, guava sweets, and assorted pastries. Guillermito and I became friends. Our favorite pastime was freestyle wrestling.

Mother sold the banana plantation and one of the houses my father had left her. She invested most of the money in cattle and gave it to my grandfather to manage for her. With the rest of the money she bought two boardinghouses in Teusaquillo, a neighborhood of faux Tudor houses. We lived in the larger house, where we had two rooms and a balcony on the third floor. One room was used as a living room where mother received friends and she sewed; the other room served as a bedroom for the three of us. Then my cousin Jorge came to study in Bogotá from El Banco, and there were four of us.

Through Fanny's recommendation I was enrolled at Washington School. The principal, Dr. Cifuentes, made a big fuss about me because of my father's name and because of my big ears. He said my ears were a sign of great intelligence and that I was destined to be president of Colombia, despite my illegitimacy.

Colombia has something of a tradition of illegitimate children who become prominent in society. The principal sent his car and driver to pick me up for school. Among the children who rode with me were the offspring of the minister of foreign affairs. Their father, Julio César Turbay Ayala, became president of Colombia in the 1970s. The other two children were the son and daughter of a senator from the State of Tolima, heirs to an important newspaper.

My love of literature was awakened at this time. A young woman named Elisa came to work at Mother's boardinghouse. She took a liking to my sister and me. Elisa was athletic, almost tomboyish. She had long hair she wore in a braid, shapely muscular legs, and alert caressing eyes. At night Elisa (who had dropped out of high school because her parents needed her to go to work) came up to our bedroom to tell us stories from the *Arabian Nights*. She also told us many of the fairy tales by Hans Christian Andersen and the Brothers Grimm. She'd put us to sleep with these stories. Elisa was a masterful storyteller, and all day long I looked forward to the moment she'd become our Scheherezade. When I closed my eyes after the lights were out for the night, my mind would be afire in the dark. I couldn't wait to grow up so I could read all those books. I began to feel intensely alive.

13

I knew there was a life beyond the physical life, a life of the mind, where the most wondrous things could take place. I was freed from the tyranny of the logic of the world, which didn't have much room for magic.

I became a bed wetter. When my mother returned from work late at night and found I had wet the bed, she'd send me downstairs to sleep with Elisa in the servants' quarters. I remember going down the stairs, late on those frigid nights, crying and dragging my soaked stinky blankets.

My asthma disappeared while we lived in Bogotá, to be replaced by other ailments. I became allergic to certain foods and would get painful rashes and swellings all over my body. A couple of times I came down with pneumonia.

Mother's establishment was home to two kinds of residents: university students and foreigners—Italians and Spaniards. An Italian named Bercelli became Mother's lover. I found Bercelli attractive. When he and my mother went into his bedroom to make love, I'd go out on the street and stand under his window, imagining them making love. He was married, but his family was still in Italy. Later, after his family arrived in Bogotá and he moved away from our boardinghouse, he'd bring his young daughter to visit us, while he made love to my mother in the adjoining room. The girl did not speak Spanish, and it was awkward to be with her, knowing what we did about our parents.

Many afternoons on the way home from school I'd fantasize that I'd find my father at home waiting for me. The fantasy was that he had come to take me away to live with his family and raise me as one of his legitimate children. That he never called to inquire about us was a source of pain.

I attended religious instruction to get ready for my first communion. The day before I received communion for the first time I found my mother in our small sitting room, at her sewing machine. As the priest had instructed us, I begged her to forgive me for the many times I had upset her and disobeyed her. I broke down and my mother embraced me. Warmly, she said that she forgave me. This is the first memory I have of my mother hugging me. I was nine.

The boardinghouses kept losing money. Frequently, Mother called my grandfather to ask him to sell some cattle for her. Many boarders skipped in the middle of the night without paying their bills. Others were too poor to pay, and Mother could not bring herself to kick them out.

Almost forty, my mother was still a beautiful woman. She became a high-class prostitute. One night she took me to the whorehouse where she worked and introduced me to a drunken American who spoke to me in English and gave me a stick of chewing gum. I felt humiliated.

The period known in Colombian history as *la violencia* was still going on. Hundreds of thousands of peasants had died in an undeclared civil war between Liberals and Conservatives. There were mass killings in the countryside just outside Bogotá. Mother would sometimes go away for weekends with military men who had haciendas in *tierra caliente* south of the savannah of Bogotá. They went there to hunt wild game and to party. Mother must have told me the name of the town or hacienda where she was going that weekend. Sunday night I was in bed listening to the radio when the news came on and the announcer said that bandoleros had entered the hacienda where Mother was staying and they had killed everyone there. What I didn't know was that Mother had left the hacienda shortly before the killings took place.

In addition to listening to Elisa's stories at night, I acquired two significant passions at that time: I fell in love with horses and betting at the racetrack; the other passion was one that would last—the movies.

Many students at Washington School were the children of the horse trainers at Bogotá's hippodrome. I became an avid follower of the races and a gambler. Many Sunday afternoons I'd go to the racetrack with my mother to bet. I often won. I may have inherited this combination of a love of animals and betting from my father, a well-known *gallero,* or breeder of fighting cocks. His *gallos de pelea* were famous throughout the Caribbean.

But the love of the movies turned out to be stronger and more lasting. On Sunday mornings I went to teatro Palermo to the kiddie shows— mostly Tarzan movies and the comedies of Abbott and Costello. Soon I started skipping school to attend the matinees by myself. I became friendly with many of the doormen of the movie theaters in Bogotá, and they'd let me go in alone. The film that affected me the most was *The African Queen.* Throughout my childhood I had recurring nightmares in which I saw Humphrey Bogart's body covered with leeches.

For my eighth birthday a friend presented me with a book, *The Adventures of Dick Turpin,* a latter-day Robin Hood. This was the first book I read from beginning to end, and from then on my hunger for books was matched only by my love of the cinema.

Despite encouragement from the principal of Washington School, I was a poor student and often got into fights with other boys. All academic subjects except history bored me. In the second grade we learned about the pre-Columbian cultures around the savannah of Bogotá. I got excellent marks in history because the stories of the Zaque and Zipa chiefs of the Chibchas, and the temples they built to the sun and the moon, and the ceremony in which El Dorado washed his gold-covered body in the lagoon of Guatavita, were tales that inflamed my imagination and made me delirious.

I had great legs. My mother invited friends over and asked me to parade around the bedroom in my underwear, showing off my legs. My mother would say, "Doesn't he have legs like Miss Universe?" and one of her friends would add something like, "If I had legs like that, I'd consider myself the luckiest woman in the world." The women cooed their agreement as they sipped coffee and nibbled on *almojábanas,* a Colombian bread I loved, and pastries. I sashayed around the bedroom, sometimes climbing on the bed to give them a better view of my gams, until the women ran out of words of praise.

Colombians were obsessed with legs. When they praised a woman's beauty, the first asset they mentioned was her legs. These discussions took place even in school. One day our music teacher told us (with great seriousness) that he felt sorry for Liz Taylor because, despite her beautiful face and tiny waist, she had no legs to speak of. He sighed, empathizing with Liz's misfortune, yet another of her tragedies! On the other hand, he added, brightening, Sophia Loren had an asymmetrical face but what legs!

In Bogotá, despite the cool climate, the boys wore short pants to school, British style. I was fully conscious of the beauty of my legs, though boys never commented on them. It was always the women who'd look at me enviously, wishing they had legs like mine to entrap and enslave their men.

There were beauty contests just for legs. The contestants paraded with hoods covering their faces and trunks to make sure that judges would not be distracted by other attributes. I would cut out the pictures of the queens of the legs, tape them on a full-length mirror, and compare their legs with mine. I thought of one day entering one of these pageants and then revealing my gender when I was crowned.

Boys stopped wearing short pants in adolescence. Meantime, I made the best possible use of my legs. I was a tall boy with long legs. Running was a popular sport in Bogotá. Because of asthma my legs were no use to me for long-distance running. But I excelled as a sprinter. I'd imagine myself a horse (a Thoroughbred with great legs) and pushed myself so hard that I won most short races I entered. My legs were also good for hiking the steep mountains right above our home. I'd climb all the way to the top and then descend on the other side to explore pristine mossy woods with crystalline rills.

I was determined to find El Dorado. I wanted to learn as much as I could about it, so one day I went to the National Museum by myself—an advantage of having strong legs was that I began to explore the city alone when I was eight. Our history teacher had mentioned the museum one day in class. It was a dark, drafty, and gloomy place made of huge cold stones. On the first floor I found a display of mummified Chibchas, their translucent skins wrapped tight around their desiccated crouching bodies, the eye sockets vacant, yellowish hair still growing on their heads, long brown teeth showing. I fled the museum, staring at the ground, unwilling to gaze at the world with eyes that now were accomplices in the terrible mystery of death. I held onto a pine tree and threw up. The mummies started haunting my dreams.

The search to find the legendary treasure of El Dorado led me to spend whole days hiking the mountains with my cousin, friends, and, occasionally, my sister. We'd climb all the way to the top of the steep and slippery mountains looking for gold. The orangy soil of the mountains looked like gold to me, and we always returned to the city loaded with rocks we hoped were made of gold. One late afternoon I became lost in a violent hailstorm and got soaked in the icy rain. I caught pneumonia and nearly died. I was in bed for weeks, hallucinating about the treasures of El Dorado.

At the base of the mountain nearest our house was Javeriana University, a Jesuit school. Often, in the late afternoon my sister, my cousin, and I would enter the morgue of the school of medicine by sliding down a slope of gravel behind the building. We'd play hide-and-seek in the morgue, hiding under the sheets that covered the mutilated corpses or in the iceboxes where many cadavers were stored.

One day Elisa informed us that her family's financial situation had improved and that she would be able to return to school to become a pharmacist. We hugged and cried. I don't remember ever crying as much. We had become so attached to her that on her days off we'd go with her to visit her parents. She would rent bicycles for us, and we'd spend the afternoons cycling. The pain I felt after she left was the sharpest and most shattering emotion I had known since Stick Luster's mother had forbidden him to see me again. The two people I had loved the most as a child were taken away from me abruptly. This left me with the dread that all my loved ones would sooner or later be taken from me in cruel ways. For many years afterward I dreamed of running into Elisa. In my teens, when I knew I'd become a writer, I realized that Elisa had fired up my mind, prodding my imagination to want to create its own stories.

Elisa was replaced by another maid, Dioselina. Now it seems clear to me that these women gave me whatever mothering I got as a boy. At first I disliked Dioselina. But soon I grew attached to her too. Dioselina, who was overweight, was not a lover of books, but she shared my passion for the movies. On her days off we'd go see movies in second-run theaters so we could go twice in the same day. We'd go to wrestling matches together. Many freezing nights we sat in the cheapest seats high up in the bullfighting arena where the matches were held. I grew to love Dioselina. I felt sorry for her because her only sister had died the year before she came to work for us in a fire at Tía, a popular convenience store in Colombia.

17

After I had my first communion, I attended mass regularly on my own. In the late 1950s Bogotá was, like Colombian society at large, medieval in its thinking. The religion teacher told us that if we died during the week without going to mass (and she would warn us that we could be squashed by a bus or truck as we crossed the streets), we would burn forever in hell—suffering the most excruciating pain imaginable. Whenever I did not make it to mass on Sunday, I experienced an insane terror whenever I had to leave the house to go anywhere.

I was growing up a wild child. My sister was a poor student, and she was constantly punished at school. I had to go get her after class to bring her home. Around Christmas time a friend and I were caught stealing toys in a department store. A store detective took us upstairs and threatened that he would announce to the customers that he had caught two thieves. He assured us that if he surrendered us to the crowds below, they would tear us apart. I knew this had happened on several occasions.

I must have been desperately trying to catch Mother's attention. I stopped eating solid foods and lost a great deal of weight. The less I ate, the less appetite I had. Friends of my mother's (the Galeanos) came to Bogotá to seek treatment for their mother, who had cancer. They stayed in our pensión. One night at dinner one of them noticed that I wasn't eating. Then she became alarmed at how skinny I looked. When they questioned me, I told them it was weeks since I had eaten any solid food. My "hunger strike" came to an end.

Several medical students boarded with us. They paid me roughly the equivalent of a quarter to let them hypnotize me for their school experiments. I was pinched with needles and burned with matches. I was wide awake throughout but pretended to be hypnotized so I could save money to go to the movies. One day one of them gave me a human heart to bite. Fully conscious, I bit into it.

This is another memory I have of those years: one of my younger uncles masturbated in front of me in an attic of the house and asked me to give him a blow job. Revolted and horrified, I wondered: Is it obvious I am a *maricón?*

Suddenly, Mother announced we were returning to Barranquilla. She placed an ad in the newspapers and put everything in the house up for sale. Overnight, beds, linen, tables, chairs, silverware—every single object of value in the house was sold.

I was unhappy to leave Bogotá, having grown to love its unremitting verdure and its mountains. I had become a *cachaco,* as people from the high

Andes are called in Colombia, and I had acquired the lilting, soft, melodious accent of the Bogotano.

We returned to Barranquilla in December. My mother was in love with Antonio Serge, a married man. He was handsome and resembled the actor Jeff Chandler. Like her Italian lover Bercelli, Antonio's hair was salt-and-pepper. My asthma returned.

During December, January, and February, Barranquilla is a lovely town. The trade winds blow from the Caribbean, sweeping through the city with great vehemence in late afternoon, cooling everything. The city's flora blooms in a potpourri of primal colors, creating a kaleidoscopic tropical spring.

My mother was having money problems. Her main source of income came from selling, one by one, the cattle that my grandfather managed for her. She sold the house in El Porvenir and handed the proceeds to Antonio Serge to manage for her. The idea was to lend money at a high interest rate and live off the borrowers' payments. Señor Antonio, as we always called him, had his own family to support. He was an unsuccessful real estate broker.

We moved into a two-bedroom apartment in downtown Barranquilla where we lived for about two years. My sister and I went to visit our father in his office in Santa Marta. For the first visit we were accompanied by Lola, Aunt Aura's mother. No bridge then connected Barranquilla with the other side of the river, and the ferry crossing was slow. My father received us coldly. He talked about Mother with bitterness and about some members of her family with contempt. He said that there was no need for us to be poor because he had left Mother enough money so we could live comfortably. He mentioned it wasn't necessary for him to acknowledge us legally as his children because we were in his will. He added that he planned to leave us half a million pesos—the dollar and the peso at that time were on par. From that moment on I began to wish for his death so we could inherit. Then he wrote a check, asked us to kiss him on the cheek, and bid us goodbye. He showed a soft spot for my sister, calling her "my *chinita*" (little Chinese one). Until we emigrated to the United States seven years later, this scenario repeated itself at least once a year, varying little from visit to visit. Over the years, though, he softened toward our mother and her family, and he warmed up to us a bit. On a couple of occasions before he went off on his annual trip to Europe, he wrote generous checks, especially when the banana crop had been good. I sensed his hostility toward me had disappeared, but I never saw a sign of affection.

I was enrolled at Colegio Colón, a lay school known in Barranquilla for its strict discipline. Troubled kids from middle-class backgrounds were sent there to be straightened out.

All my young life I had felt profoundly alienated from the world and its institutions. But the years that began now were perhaps the unhappiest of my life. Outside the school I struck a friendship with Jacobo, a Jewish boy from Bogotá who lived across the hall from us. He was staying with his aunt and uncle, childless Jews from Poland. I've gone through most of my life thinking of myself as a Jew, thinking about converting to Judaism. My closest friends have been Jews. Maybe this is because Hebrew was the first language I learned. When my novel *Colombian Gold* was published and translated into Hebrew, it seemed to me that I was finally translated into my mother tongue.

Jacobo attended Colegio Hebreo Unión (the school I had attended before our move to Bogotá but that had become too expensive for us). On Saturdays Jacobo took me to the Jewish club to swim in the pool and watch the Esther Williams movies that were usually shown. My friendship with Jacobo (he was blonde like my first love, Stick Luster) made up for the fact that school was sheer torture for me. The prefect was a brutal sadistic man named Portacio, who relished giving military punishment to the students: long sets of push-ups, or marching or standing on the spot for hours under Barranquilla's scalding sun.

Often I would get out of these punishments by faking asthma attacks. Sometimes the attacks were real. This did not ingratiate me with my classmates. Because of my Bogotano accent, and because I was a dreamy kid, the other students tormented me. They made constant jokes about my big ears, calling me Dumbo. I was overweight and the target of many jokes. One of my saddest memories is of staying in the classroom during recess. I sat at my desk and cried inconsolably while the students taunted me through the window, calling me maricón and other epithets.

Though I loved Jacobo, I couldn't share these things with him (I didn't know how). One day I decided to circumcise myself with a razor blade. Because I was uncut, I had come to believe I was a freak. I started slicing my foreskin but became horrified when I drew blood.

Colegio Colón had a small library of stuffed birds and ancient, musty, leather-bound books. There I read *Aesop's Fables,* my first "serious" book. This was another watershed moment in my life. I found *Aesop's Fables* wise and unaccountable. Nothing had fired my imagination in the same way since Elisa's stories from *The Arabian Nights*. I read everything that fell into my hands. Every day, I read two newspapers.

Jacobo and his family loved the movies. Many nights I'd accompany them to the open-air, second-run theaters of downtown Barranquilla. Steve

Reeves movies were a favorite. *Solomon and the Queen of Sheba,* starring Yul Brynner and Gina Lollobrigida, was the first steamy movie I saw.

A friend of Mother's gave us a dog. I named her Turpina, after Dick Turpin. She became the center of my sister's and my life. One night Mother and Señor Antonio went to the movies, and I woke up to find the apartment full of smoke and my mother bathing an unconscious Turpina in the bathroom. A fire had started while they were away, and they had returned just in the nick of time.

I pestered my mother for money to go to the movies all the time. One day Mother became so incensed she smashed my head against the corrugated wall of the hall and my forehead split. I had to be taken to the hospital for stitches. I still have a bump on the upper left corner of my forehead.

Our apartment had two bedrooms—a small one near the front door, where I slept, and a large bedroom with two beds that my mother and sister shared. Señor Antonio usually stayed until midnight and then left to spend the rest of the night at his home. Only on weekends did he stay the whole night. It was around this time that I began to watch Mother and Señor Antonio make love. Usually, after he left, when I woke up to find my bed wet, I'd move to my mother's bed and sleep with her till morning. One night when I was eleven, I woke up holding my mother in my arms, and I was fully aroused. I had the impression we had been kissing passionately, that we had just finished making love. I felt enormous guilt and shame, like the guilt and shame I imagined Adam and Eve experienced after making love and being expelled from Paradise.

We moved to a pretty house in Barrio Boston with three bedrooms and a backyard. It was our home until we emigrated to the United States. I began to hold and judge beauty pageants at home, drawing a pool of contestants from my sister's friends. The girl with the best legs always won. My sister won one day—great legs ran in the family. I was not interested in the girls as objects of desire, but my appreciation of shapely legs had turned me into an aesthete.

Our family was doing better financially. Señor Antonio was named director of the state brewery, one of the most important jobs in the city because the brewery is one of the state's main sources of revenue. A perk was a green Cadillac with a uniformed chauffeur. Often he entertained some of his politician friends at our home. Once, I remember, he put me on the phone while he was talking to Guillermo Valencia, then president of Colombia.

I managed to communicate to my mother my great unhappiness about Colegio Colón and was transferred to Colegio Americano, the school that had expelled me for asking the boy in kindergarten to show me his penis—they had forgotten who I was. I learned then that time can erase many memories, even unpleasant ones. I entered *primero de bachillerato,* the equivalent of the ninth grade.

From then until we moved to the States, the years were divided between school in Barranquilla and vacation in El Banco. I was sent to visit my mother's relatives in the country to make sure that I spent time with my cowboy uncles doing manly things and thus become "a man." At first I dreaded leaving the city for El Banco. The hot dusty town is situated on the shores of the Magdalena River, deep in the countryside of the Atlantic coast. Usually, I stayed with my aunt Emilia, my godmother. Other times, I stayed at my grandfather's house. At that point my grandfather had three farms: Las Marías, La Esperanza, and Tosnován. Las Marías was on the outskirts of El Banco, a mere half-hour walk from the house. La Esperanza was on the shores of the Magdalena, several hours from the town by boat. Tosnován was in *tierra templada* in the temperate zone of the Andes, two days' journey from El Banco.

At my grandfather's house lived my two young aunts who went to school in Bogotá and five unmarried uncles. I bonded with Uncle Hernán, the youngest, with whom I spent many afternoons and nights hunting. He was interested in radical politics, and through him I heard about socialism and Marxism for the first time. Years later, when I read Ivan Turgenev's *Sketches from a Hunter's Album,* I was astounded by the similarities between the Russian countryside in the nineteenth century and Colombia's in the middle of the twentieth—the Russian serfs reminded me of our Colombian peasants. Those afternoons are among the most indelible memories of my adolescence—the scorching sun on our backs while Uncle Hernán looked for game birds, with me trailing him and carrying his rifle. The countryside, however, was a dangerous place: bad-tempered scorpions hid in your pockets and shoes, mighty anacondas hung from trees ready to crush your ribcage and gobble you up, and brilliant poisonous vipers sunned on the rocks, baring their needle-sharp fangs dripping with deadly venom. The lagoons where I swam with Hernán teamed with caymans (a relative of the alligator) that could maim or drown you, sting rays that could paralyze you, and voracious leeches that could drain you of all your blood. In addition to the *collongos* (cranes) and *piscingos* (ducks) that Hernán shot for Mamá Berta's table, we hunted iguanas for their eggs, piercing the side of their bellies, tearing out strings of pulpy white eggs, and then tossing the bleeding animal into the bush. I knew that the iguanas would not die, that this had been going on for ages, but even though I was reassured they felt no pain, it seemed barbaric. The countryside abounded with wild animals: monkeys, sloths, armadillos, deer, ñeques, guartinajas, morrocoyos, and bobcats, all animals of the rain forest. Except for the cats, all these animals made it to the dinner table. The river yielded plentiful harvests of the prehistoric-looking bagres (the size of dolphins), catfish, coroncoros, tiny sardines, lebranches, lisas. The array of fruits was equally impressive: guamas, corozos (from which a sweet juice—a rich red wine that was almost an elixir—was made), anones, nísperos, ciruelas, mameys, zapotes, the juicy fruit of the cashew tree, *perillas,* many kinds of mangoes, guanábanas, pineapples, coconuts, tamarind, papayas, guavas, icacos, mamones, and many varieties of bananas and plantains. Exquisite juices, sweets, and cakes were made from all these.

I also bonded with my younger aunts, who read books and loved the movies. At night the family sat on the sidewalk to enjoy the evening breeze, and there I would hold court, narrating in minute detail the best new movies I had seen in Barranquilla during the school year. A few nights a week I accompanied my aunts to the local movie theaters. One night I saw *The Blue Angel,* starring Marlene Dietrich. It was an old scratchy print, but I was perfectly aware of seeing for the first time something that spoke to me about the mystery and power of sex. It was both scary and thrilling. Dietrich seemed to beckon me and whisper, "Come, and I'll give you pleasures so rich you won't mind dying for them." She didn't seem particularly feminine but an embodiment of the ecstasies that the body held.

I dreaded some aspects of life in El Banco. Occasionally, I was reminded by one of my aunts or uncles that I was not a real part of the family and did not belong there. Dramas were constantly unraveling, the family resembling a nest of scorpions feeding off each other. My grandfather's tantrums and rages were monumental. One time my mother came to visit. I misbehaved, and my mother locked me in the room where they kept the saddles. When I would not quiet down, she took one of her high heels and cracked my forehead open. I bled profusely. Mother's family was an extremely unhappy clan. My grandfather, a tyrant, terrorized his children, sometimes breaking their wills for the rest of their lives.

I could not compete with my cousins in swimming the rivers and lagoons, lassoing cows and milking them, racing horses, helping to stamp the cattle with hot irons, or fucking all the animals in sight: chickens, pigs and, above all, the female donkeys. In my forties, reading Reinaldo Arenas's autobiography, I learned that our adolescence in the tropical countryside had many points in common.

I heard stories about witchcraft. The people of the region were observant Catholics, but their imaginations were animistic and they believed in the evil eye, in the creatures of the forest that were manifestations of the devil and his allies. My grandfather would entertain us with tales of the witches he had caught as animals and then had seen transformed into women again. He claimed to have supernatural powers and we all believed—and feared—him.

Back in Barranquilla life was more complicated. I hated school, was undisciplined, never did my homework, was bored with most subjects, hated math, and I didn't care for my teachers or most classmates.

I was interested only in the movies and reading books. And, a little later, in writing. At Colegio Americano I became friends in the ninth grade with Luis Díaz Barros, who would remain my close friend until he died of AIDS in New York twenty-five years later. One day, I fell asleep in class. The teacher said, "Marmot, wake up!" and from then on, my classmates taunted me calling me *marmota*.

Luis Díaz was an island in the middle of the sea of insensitivity I found myself in. His mother was a secretary for Postobón, one of the largest soda companies in Colombia. He lived with his brother, mother, and grandmother in a lower middle-class neighborhood. We became inseparable. Shy, unathletic, bookish, we were different from the other boys. We both wanted to be writers. We started composing poems and short stories, which we mailed off on a weekly basis to the literary magazines of the newspapers in Bogotá. We enrolled in English classes at the Assa Institute, and twice a week after school, we walked more than forty blocks to Professor Assa's. These afternoon walks with Luis were sheer happiness. Along the way, we sometimes stopped at Colegio San José, a Catholic school, to discuss theology with the priests. We were determined to show the fallacies in Christian theology. On Saturdays I'd go to Luis's house where we'd spend the day playing chess and reading *Hamlet* and other plays under a guava tree in his backyard.

The nature of our friendship made my mother uneasy. She disliked Luis's effeminate ways and tried to discourage me from spending so much time with him. The biology teacher at Colegio Americano despised me and spread the rumor that Luis and I were lovers. Though we both turned out to be gay, at that time we had no language to talk about these things. Besides, I was not attracted to him. Luis was a chubby nerd, wore huge thick glasses, and was effeminate.

I was in love with Eugenio Maya. Eugenio was the handsomest boy at school—he was tall, with hyacinth-black hair and onyx eyes; he had the looks of a sensitive-looking Rock Hudson. His father was a Baptist minister, and the family had recently moved to Barranquilla from the United States. They were Puerto Rican. Eugenio was not interested in the arts, but he was sweet-tempered and he must have enjoyed my attentions. All the girls adored him.

He'd come to sleep over, and I'd climb into his bed, take out his erect penis, and stroke it. Then I would lay my head on his stomach, and I would kiss or lick his warm sweet skin. He always pretended to sleep through all this, but he never missed an opportunity to sleep with me in the same room or in the same bed.

So many things began to happen at once: sex, writing, the love of literature, a deepening of my interest in the movies. There was no time to think about school, which was dull by comparison. Our next-door neighbors had a collection of leather-bound books called *The Great Novels of World Literature.* I began to read them with a zealousness that nothing has evoked since. The collection included the great novelists of the nineteenth century. I read Dostoyevski's *Crime and Punishment,* which made such an impression I kept it under my pillow; *Anna Karenina* and *Resurrection* by Tolstoy; Turgenev's *Sons and Fathers* and *Sketches from a Hunter's Album.* Physically, I lived in Barranquilla, but my mind was full of nineteenth-century Russia. This changed when I read *Jane Eyre* and, more important, *Wuthering Heights,* which I reread eighteen times. I'd walk Barranquilla's hot streets and imagine myself exploring the wild melancholy moors of England. I wanted to die of consumption, like the Brontës. I sat in my chair at school, in the back of the classroom, and coughed all day long, hoping that way to develop consumption. And then I read Flaubert's *Madame Bovary,* which I read over and over, until I moved on to *Bouvard et Pécuchet,* which, to me, read like a strange homosexual love story. I devoured Stendhal's *The Red and the Black,* Balzac's *Père Goriot* and *Eugénie Grandet,* Dickens's *Oliver Twist* and *David Copperfield,* Thackeray's *Vanity Fair* (which had an enchantingly evil heroine whose dreams of social climbing I shared), and George Elliot's *The Mill on the Floss,* a novel close to my heart because the bond between Maggie and her brother reminded me of my bond with my sister.

It's quite possible I might not have become a writer if my neighbors had not owned this collection and been gracious enough to lend me these books. When I look back, though, nothing that's happened to me since has marked me as profoundly as the reading of these works. I lived through Anna Karenina and Madame Bovary and Oliver Twist and Raskolnikov. I lived in their societies, and in their drawing rooms, and I was happy when they experienced joy and suffered when they suffered.

When I wasn't reading, I was going to the movies. Next door to our house was Teatro Buenos Aires, an open-roof movie theater. A few times a week my mother and Señor Antonio went to the movies. I would time it so that, after they entered the theater, I'd follow them and sit a few rows behind. I had become friends with the ticket taker, who would let me in for free. A double feature was shown every night, so I would leave after the first movie was over. At that time movies arrived in Barranquilla indiscriminately. I saw everything: European and Hollywood and Mexican and Spanish films. Hollywood movies were my favorite. Movies about cowboys and Indians, comedies starring Doris Day and Rock Hudson, the "adult" films of Elizabeth Taylor, musicals (which Barranquilleros hated—whenever a character broke into song and dance a minor riot ensued in the movie theater). The first film my sister and I awaited with anxiety was *Psycho*. When it opened, our Uncle Chelo took us to see it and for weeks afterward we had nightmares. Taking a shower became a scary act.

I loved the big spectacles: *Ben Hur* and *Spartacus,* but the first movie that affected me with a power that I had thought only books could have was Vittorio De Sica's *Two Women,* starring Sophia Loren. The rape scene haunted me for a long time, a reminder of the evil that is rampant in the world.

The great European films of the early sixties hit our local theaters. I had a friend in school, Eduardo Cabesas, who was also a movie buff, and he introduced me to a friend of his, a woman who was almost fifteen years our senior. She lived with an older man, but she and Eduardo were good friends. Her name is Josefina Folgoso, and she and I established a relationship that has lasted for more than thirty-five years. Josefina took us under her wing and introduced us to Fellini's *La Dolce Vita,* Truffaut's *Jules et Jim,* Goddard's *Breathless,* Luchino Visconti's *The Leopard* and *Rocco and His Brothers.*

Josefina also introduced me to European and American contemporary writers: Françoise Sagan, Jean Paul Sartre, Hemingway, Simone de Beauvoir, Henry Miller, Nabokov. She passed on to me a set of novels that made a huge impression (asking me to read them in four days and warning me that these were "special books"), Lawrence Durrell's *The Alexandrian Quartet.* The more I read and went to the movies, the more alienated I felt from school and most of my peers.

My uncle Giovanni, who had a bad limp, came to live with us. He was a handsome young man in his late twenties (which to me was old). I was attracted to him. We shared the same bedroom. Giovanni was in the city to try to get a job as a secretary (he had gone to secretarial school), but he didn't seem to have luck landing any kind of work. At night, before going to bed, I'd watch him undress and put on his pajamas—he wore only the pants. I'd go to bed feeling thoroughly aroused.

There was a *sereno* (watchman) in our neighborhood who'd patrol the streets at night to make sure no burglars were trying to break into the houses—something that was common in Barranquilla. Often, the burglars took our chickens. Starting at ten o'clock, the sereno would blow a whistle every hour on the hour to indicate that everything was in order. Then I'd crawl to my mother's room and watch her and Señor Antonio make love. In retrospect, it seems that they made love passionately every night. I lived for their lovemaking at night, often masturbating while they had sex. Then one night I became bolder, and instead of going to my mother's room, I crawled to the other side of my room where Giovanni slept. I put my hand on his crotch. He had a hard-on. I took his cock out of his pajamas and held it in my hand. But I had no idea what to do with his penis, now that I had gotten a hold of it. Night after night I'd go over to Giovanni's bed and stroke his hard penis. I'd smell it, fascinated with the acrid smell that emanated from it, then I'd place it next to my cheeks and stroke it tenderly. This went on for most of my thirteenth year. Whenever I saw Giovanni during the day, I'd close my eyes and imagine his cock in my hand, my lips touching the tip of its head. When we went for rides in Uncle Chelo's jeep, I'd sit next to Giovanni and try to press my body against his. He seemed repelled by my advances even as he tolerated them.

Other than those late night skirmishes, Giovanni and I never had contact of any kind. One night I was returning home after my English class, and I saw him sitting on the terrace, reading the newspaper. As I was entering the house, he looked up and said, "Marilyn Monroe killed herself." These were the first words he had spoken directly to me in a long time, perhaps years. He seemed devastated. I ran into the house and turned the radio on and, yes, it was on the news. That night, as usual, I got up from my bed late at night to worship his penis. As I touched it, he grabbed my hand and barked at me, "You had better stop doing that or I'm gonna tell Soledad." I went back to my bed, shaken, terrified. From that moment on I began to live in terror that Giovanni would tell my mother what I had been doing for months.

I came to terms with my homosexuality slowly. I did not come out of the closet until I was in my midtwenties (but I was full of internalized homophobia until I was in my midthirties). Guilt ran my life from my adolescence on. Guilt and secrecy. *The Trials of Oscar Wilde,* starring Peter Finch, arrived in Barranquilla. It focused on the circumstances that led to Wilde's destruction as a man and as an artist. A classmate had a library that contained *The Complete Works of Oscar Wilde.* I borrowed the bulky volumes and read them in a couple of weeks. I couldn't yet appreciate the great wit of the plays, the scalpel-sharp intelligence of the criticism, nor the originality of the fairy tales. Instead, I was fascinated with *The Portrait of Dorian Gray* and *Salome,* works that expressed murky and dangerous sensuality. But the work with which I identified the most was the poem Wilde wrote from jail. I learned by heart entire passages of *The Ballad of Reading Gaol.* I became terrified of my deepening homosexual feelings. Wilde's story seemed a warning of what happened to men who transgressed the boundaries of heterosexual society: they ended up in jail and they were destroyed physically, socially, and spiritually.

Barranquilla had one public homosexual, who was nicknamed "Tarzan." He was notorious for preying on adolescents. He was an outcast and an object of ridicule. When he went by my house, strutting his impressive musculature, I was repelled by him, although I wanted his knowledge of men. I put together the two images of homosexuality I knew—Oscar Wilde and Tarzan—and I thought this meant I was doomed to a life of ostracism.

I started to write more earnestly. My first literary efforts were about rain, fog, death, meaninglessness, suicide, nothingness, *la nada.* I was faced with this dilemma: how to write about my deepest feelings without risking persecution. Writing therefore became a terrible struggle to express and censor at the same time. I realized that writing was, in my case, a risky activity because of what I might expose about me.

During these years the bond with my sister grew more intense. Now, in retrospect, I can see that we were perhaps terrified of what the future, adulthood, held for us. We went to the movies constantly. Our beloved dog Turpina was the focus of our life. One day, I awoke to screams in the house. I rushed from bed and learned that Turpina had been poisoned. My mother tried desperately to safe her life by pouring milk down her throat, trying to get her to throw up. But Turpina died in the midst of harrowing convulsions: foaming at the mouth, yelping in pain, shitting all over my mother, the dog's soft hazel eyes pregnant with terror.

That night Giovanni dug a hole under a mango tree in the backyard to bury Turpina. Barranquilla's custom was to throw dead dogs into an empty lot, but my sister and I opposed this violently. We cried inconsolably, having lost a pet that always met us leaping with joy whenever we arrived home from school. I remember that for months afterward my heartbroken sister cried at night in her bed, so loudly that a neighbor, a kind young woman, would come to console her. Then one day I overheard someone in our house insinuate that perhaps Turpina had been poisoned by Giovanni. It seems quite possible that this was his way of getting even with me. Shortly after that he left and went back to my grandfather's house.

I found that I had a talent for reciting poetry and started entering the concursos de declamación, a series of poetry performances for adolescents that was held in Barranquilla. These contests were the equivalent of today's poetry slams, except that instead of reciting our own poems, we declaimed, among others, the poetry of Federico García Lorca, the Colombians Porfirio Barba Jacob and José Asunción Silva, and the Chilean Nobel laureate Gabriela Mistral—all queer poets, with the exception of Silva. I was, however, ignorant of the sexuality of the poets I loved. My favorites were Silva and Porfirio Barba Jacob. Silva's "Nocturno," with his emphasis on death, madness, and despair, spoke directly to me. And Barba Jacob's *Canción de la vida profunda* has lines that suggest a dissolute life and that hint at why he was considered our scandalous poet. But the poet most widely performed was Federico García Lorca. *Lament for Ignacio Sánchez Mejías,* "The Death of Little Tony Camborio," and "Sleepwalking Ballad," poems with rapturous rhymes and lush romantic use of Spanish folklore, were favorites in the concursos de declamación. Whether we performed his poetry or not, we had all heard of his tragic death at the hands of General Franco's fascist sympathizers during the Spanish Civil War. The fate of García Lorca the martyr seemed to me so terrible, and made such an impression, that I swore I would not set foot in Spain as long as General Francisco Franco lived—a vow I kept. I visited Spain for the first time in January 1977, two months after the hated dictator's death.

I was not a fan of García Lorca's poetry. For my friend Luis Díaz and me, García Lorca's *Gypsy Ballads* were objects of mockery. If we wanted to break into peals of laughter, all we had to do was to say the opening lines of "Sleepwalking Ballad":

> *Verde que te quiero verde.*
> *Verde viento. Verdes ramas.*
>
> Green oh how I love you green.
> Green wind. Green boughs.

We would articulate *verrrrrde,* rolling the Rs with extreme exaggeration, which caused us endless amusement. What we snotty adolescents were reacting to in García Lorca's poetry was the old-fashioned rhymes and the conventional feelings expressed. To us, avant-garde youngsters, these poems seemed unmodern, silly, corny. Federico García Lorca was everything we wanted to rebel against as writers. However, the poems were popular with performers, I assume, because of their musicality and the dramatic possibilities they offered—through rhymes and repetitions and a strong narrative—for great theatricality. It was a safe way of being a drag queen without having to cross-dress.

I was the class clown, a poor student, and kept getting into trouble at school. One day I openly mocked a teacher. He complained to the prefect, and I was suspended from school. I knew that my mother would be upset. I was afraid of punishment. I wanted sympathy; I wanted to be understood. So I decided to attempt suicide. I wrote a note to the school principal and handed it to Luis Díaz and explained to him what I was about to do. I asked him to follow me to the veranda on the second floor, which was perhaps eighteen feet high. I knew that I would not die from the fall, but I hoped I would break a leg and then all would be forgiven. In any case, I was not afraid of suicide. Both Luis and I had read Camus and considered suicide the only legitimate philosophical question. I sat on the rail of the veranda and then became afraid. I couldn't go through with it. The height scared me. I was about to change my mind when Luis pushed me. I fell and landed on my legs. Then I collapsed. I remember hearing Luis running down the hall and screaming that I had tried to kill myself. The pain was excruciating. Eventually, an ambulance arrived and I was taken to a nearby hospital. I hoped I was paralyzed. I didn't want to deal with the world, life, and its responsibilities ever again. The doctors examined me and took x-rays. They determined that I had cracked two vertebrae but that I would be able to walk again.

My mother heard the news of my suicide attempt on the radio. I was put in a cast, and several days later I was sent home. It was doubtful that I would finish the school year. The exams were just a couple of months away. Luis Díaz did not call to apologize for pushing me, and he never came by to see me. Other friends did. Eugenio, who was getting ready to move to the States, came every day at lunchtime and kept me company. We talked about his impending trip, about which he was quite excited. As the day of his departure neared, I began to suffer intensely. Then the day arrived. As a parting gift, I gave him a new shirt that a relative had given me as a present. Eugenio liked the shirt and this made me happy. Many years later I saw clearly that perhaps I had tried to somehow prevent him from leaving me. Eugenio wrote to me from Georgia a few times, then the letters stopped. In the late sixties I heard he had been killed in Vietnam.

I was able to return to school to take the finals. I wore a cast and leaned on a cane for support. I barely passed. Colegio Americano asked me not to come back the following year.

I was more isolated than ever. Eugenio had left, Luis Díaz did not show his face, and only Josefina and Luis Cera (the boy who had loaned me the Oscar Wilde books) came to visit. At the end of December, when I was finally able to leave the house with the help of a cane, the neighborhood kids called me Superman, because I had tried to fly. The English movie *A Taste of Honey* was playing at Teatro Metro and I went to see it. It was the story of a teenager, Jo, a lonely ugly duckling played by Rita Tushingham. Jo is a painter who clowns to mask her anguish. Her mother, Helen, played by Dorita Bryan, is a fading alcoholic singer who mistreats Jo and who cares only about the men she dates. Jo is a klutz, and she wanders the wet bleak streets of Liverpool the way I used to wander the streets of Barranquilla for hours. She's kept late in school. But Jo has a sharp tongue, she's witty, and she believes she's "geniused," and "an extraordinary person." Jo meets a black sailor-cook, Jimmy, and she gets pregnant. Helen kicks her out. One day Jo meets Geoff, an effeminate gentle homosexual, and they become best friends. They create their own utopia, setting up house and playing at being adults. Geoff fancies himself the father of Jo's child. Yet Jo does not want to be a mother; she does not want to grow up to become a woman; she's afraid of the responsibilities of adulthood. She rebuffs Geoff's affection. He tells her, "You need somebody to love you while you're looking for someone to love." Eventually, Helen finds Jo, moves in, and kicks Geoff out. At the end of the movie Jo, hugely pregnant, stands in a depressing alley, holding a lighted sparkler, while slum children play in the background.

I saw the movie many times. Geoff was the first homosexual I had seen portrayed as a loving human being on the screen, or anywhere, for that matter. And I identified completely with Jo. Like her, I felt I was a misunderstood genius, and like her I longed to take control of my life. One night, after a terrible row with my mother, I packed my copy of *Crime and Punishment* in my suitcase, grabbed my cane, and left the house. I had no idea where I would go. I had a friend, Leida, a girl who liked me the way I was. I thought if I went to live with her we would re-create Jo and Geoff's relationship. When I got to the corner of my block, I remembered that Leida was already married and expecting a child. And I was in too much pain to take another step. I could barely stand on my own legs.

I returned to Colegio Colón the following year and I became an artist. I was wary about returning to a school where I had been unhappy but glad for the opportunity to have a fresh start in a place where my new classmates were not aware of my failed "suicide attempt."

Teachers have been important in my life. At Colegio Colón I met a mentor who had a major influence on my development. His name was Profesor Alvaro Rincón. He must have been in his late twenties and he was a student of literature at a local university. He was dark, handsome, tall, and beefy, and his two upper front teeth were missing. I had a crush on him, though Profesor Rincón was heterosexual and dated the principal's assistant, whom he later married.

Profesor Rincón taught literature with a missionary zeal. He talked about the authors we read in a way that made them alive and vital people. We read García Márquez's *In Evil Hour* and *Leaf Storm,* books that signaled something innovative in Colombian literature. Profesor Rincón would talk about the latest art movies that had arrived in the city. I wanted to write stories and essays and to excel in his class just to please him. I wanted—badly needed—his approval. One day he gave me a book by André Gide in which the French writer described visiting Moroccan male whorehouses accompanied by Oscar Wilde. Profesor Rincón handed me the book, saying, "You might like this." He gave it to me after class, in secrecy, as if he knew that he was doing something forbidden. I read it, thrilled by the lurid sexual activities that Gide described and returned the book without saying a word. But I understood why he had given me that book to read: he knew about my love of men, and this was his way of saying, "Look, these great writers were like you. It is okay."

I had read Oscar Wilde's plays, many of the plays by García Lorca, and a play by a Colombian nadaista, Fanny Buitrago, a writer from Barranquilla whose work I loved. The nadaistas were Colombia's version of the French existentialists, and as the name suggests, they believe nothingness is the essence of the universe. I wrote a play, *¿En manos de quién?* (In whose hands?). I remember little of the plot, except that it was an existential drama about an atheist who tries to find meaning in the universe. Each scene closed with a song by the Beatles and the main characters dancing to the song. (I adored the Beatles. I'd listen to their albums and dance with my sister to their music for hours.) I enlisted my friend Miriam to play the female role. Next I convinced the school administration to finance a performance. I booked the auditorium of the Teatro de Bellas Artes, and invitations went out to other high schools in the city. The afternoon of the performance, the theater was full. The play began; whenever an actor would lose his place in the script, I'd run backstage and play a Beatles song and we'd dance for a while. The public cheered wildly. In the audience that day was a famous newspaper columnist in Barranquilla. The next day he wrote a piece about the play, praising its originality and calling me a brilliant young author. (I didn't use my name—I had signed it Q-30-77, or something like that. As an avant-garde playwright, I did not believe in names. I was copying the nadaistas. One of their most famous poets was X-504. I wanted to identify myself as a man of the future.) Overnight I became a celebrity at school and among kids in Barranquilla. During the monthly ceremony to raise the Colombian flag, the school conferred upon me the highest honor—to raise the flag while the school band played the national anthem. It was the sweetest moment of my life to that point.

Now I knew that I would become a published author. Josefina took me to see Luis Buñuel's *Diary of a Chambermaid,* and I wrote a review of it that appeared on the front page of the school newspaper, which I edited. The review caused a stir. My teachers said that it was too good to have been written by a young person. This disbelief in what I had done was the greatest praise I had yet received. Emboldened by my successes, I started my first novel, *The Void,* an existential narrative of undigested Sartre and Camus. I became a popular kid, full of self-confidence. I even started getting good grades.

One day Mother announced that she had received her visa permit to move to the United States as a resident alien. By now our finances had improved and our home was almost luxurious. Mother was still living with Señor Antonio, who had been reelected to his post as head of the state brewery. What I didn't know was that their relationship was cooling off, that he had set up house with a young woman who had been his secretary, a woman who was twenty-five years younger than my mother. Though Mother was still a beautiful woman, at forty-five she had begun to lose her appeal to many men. She saw clearly what was happening: Señor Antonio would leave her for the young woman, just as my father had left her for a much younger lover. Her great beauty had been Mother's main asset in terms of getting a man and keeping him. She had not even finished primary school. She did not have a good head for making investments, always trusting the wrong people. Perhaps she thought that in the United States she might be able to get a job that could support her and her children.

One day, just as she had in Bogotá several years earlier, she put up everything for sale and overnight we had nothing but our beds. She was coming to New York to work as a maid for a family that had given her the papers so she could get a resident visa.

It was the end of the school year. Mother left for New York, and my sister and I were shipped off to El Banco. Before leaving, my mother sublet a couple of rooms of the house, and my mother's goddaughter, Anastasia, stayed in the house with her two small children.

The plan was that as soon as Mother settled in New York my sister and I would join her. We went to stay with my aunt Maruja and her family.

They had eight children. Maruja's husband, Moisés, disliked me. I'm sure I wasn't easy to get along with—I was opinionated and disrespectful. I often fought with my male cousins. One day I said something at the dinner table that Moisés didn't like, and he asked us to leave his house that day. I went with my sister to stay at our grandfather's home.

I felt awful. Although we had a roof over our heads, we were homeless. Mother was in the States, our father was in Europe (he wouldn't have had anything to do with us in any event). One of my half-brothers, Jesús, was in charge of sending us our monthly allowance. I called him from El Banco and he sent us seven hundred pesos, which we spent on a dress for my sister for Christmas Eve. I designed the dress. I wanted her to look like Stefania Sandrelli, an actress we both liked.

Desolate, feeling adrift in the world, unwanted in my mother's family, we'd go by the town's wharf and sit there late in the afternoon and console each other as best we could.

It was apparent to me that my uncle Hernán wanted to have sex with my sister, who was barely thirteen. I tried to prevent it as much as I could, making sure that they were never alone. But many nights I was terrified that he would rape her. That Christmas and New Year's Eve was a horrible time for my sister and me. Then, as New Year's approached, and many family members went back to the cities where they lived, it was decided that my sister should go stay with my aunt Emilia and her family in Cúcuta. It was suggested that I stay in El Banco and go to school there. It seemed a fate worse than death. I was just barely sixteen, but I made up my mind I'd return to Barranquilla to live on my own. Nobody tried to stop me. I don't think anybody could have. I don't think anybody cared. I decided to return to our house in Barrio Boston, where strangers lived now. One room had not been sublet.

I took the bus back to Barranquilla, then a daylong trip. A family of strangers was living in my bedroom: a young woman, her mother, and her son. I took my sister's room. The year before I had started a correspondence with a schoolteacher in Bogotá. He sent me his picture: he looked small and blondish and a bit like the actor who played Geoff in *A Taste of Honey*. I considered running away to Bogotá to live with him. I sent him my picture. We were exchanging letters of love without mentioning the word.

But I felt muddled. I was living on the allowance that my half-brother forwarded to me. The world that I had known just a few months earlier had changed drastically. In six weeks or so school would begin and I was living alone. I am not quite clear about the events that unfolded next. As I remember, I may have had a bad headache and took several pills before going to bed. I woke up the next day in the hospital. My uncle Chelo was there. Gently, he told me that I had been found unconscious by the people living in our home. He said I had tried to kill myself again.

I had a terrible infection in my testicles, some kind of horrible venereal disease that I had caught, probably while fucking donkeys with Uncle Hernán. I was in a lot of pain and weak and distraught. My father had returned from Europe and came to see me at the hospital. He assumed all financial responsibility. I don't remember what was said during his visit. No mention was made of my second suicide attempt. My father looked at me with puzzlement. Obviously, I was a problem and he wanted no part of it.

When I was discharged from the hospital, Uncle Chelo and his wife (they had married the year before) took me to live with them in their new apartment. I had my own room where I convalesced, reading books and the letters that kept arriving from my friend. I was too weak to leave the apartment, but when I did I began to think seriously about joining my "boyfriend" in Bogotá who kept inviting me to come to live with him.

My mother returned from New York, and I moved back to our house and my sister arrived from Cúcuta. We were seriously poor. Señor Antonio and my mother were through as lovers. She had lost his financial support. We had no furniture. School started, but I was ashamed to invite my friends to come over to the house. My sister had only one worn-out uniform for school. She'd wash it at night and starch it and iron it in the morning. We lived on what my father sent us plus whatever other money my mother managed to get her hands on. Mother bought a take-out lunch every day that we divided three ways. I started doing poorly in school again. I put all my energy into finishing my novel, *The Void*. Whatever else was going on around me, I knew this: I was a writer.

Mother decided to return to the United States. She had a friend, Lucy López, who lived in Lakeland, Florida, with her husband and their children. They started a correspondence and Lucy invited us to come live with her. We started preparing for our trip. My sister would move in with Uncle Chelo until we could send for her. My mother still had her resident visa. I applied for a student visa, which I got without trouble because my father sponsored me. Right before we left I went to Santa Marta to visit my father in his office. Again he received me coldly. He wrote a check for fifty dollars and told me he hoped I would never again come to him for money.

We flew to Miami, then took another plane to Tampa, where we arrived late that night. We took a taxi and arrived in Lakeland well after midnight. Lucy and Armando, her husband, and their eight children lived in a small three-bedroom house. Armando, who was of Cuban descent but born in Tampa, worked as a draftsman for an engineering company. Lakeland, which is an in-land community, reminded me of the town that is the setting for *To Kill a Mockingbird*. I was enrolled at Lakeland High, where Patty, the oldest daughter of the family, was a senior.

That year, 1967, was the year Lakeland High School was integrated. I shall never forget my first day of classes in this country. I was trying to find the school cafeteria during lunch hour when I ran into a pack of black and white students, screaming. Two boys—one blond, one black—were battling viciously, like fighting roosters intent on drawing blood. They startled wrangling, their heads locking. One boy produced a long, piercing howl, and I saw the blond boy clasp his head desperately with both hands. Then I noticed on the other boy's lips a chunk of flesh, a bleeding piece of ear.

I knew about the brutality of the Ku Klux Klan. As a boy I had read *Uncle Tom's Cabin*. I had felt deep humiliation when my father had alluded to my father's family as Negroes, but nothing had prepared me for the horror of that moment. I knew right away I had arrived in a society where racial conflict was a matter of life and death, not a submerged issue, the way it was in Colombia, where blacks were invisible and voiceless.

Only a dozen or so black students were enrolled at Lakeland High. Many white kids were friendly toward me, but I instinctively hung out with the blacks. During lunch hour I'd sit at their table; on the school bus I sat next to them. I loved their music: I adored James Brown and the Supremes.

I was put in the twelfth grade, so graduation was just six months away. I knew enough English that I understood what was going on in the classes and within a month I could do my homework.

Because Lakeland was a small southern town without much of a Latino population, and my mother spoke no English, she had to start looking for work elsewhere. She found a job in St. Petersburg, a couple of hours away by car. She went to work for a Cuban family, taking care of an old woman, the mother of the mistress of the house. I found work after school in a downtown hotel for retired people. I ran the manual elevator and was paid fifty cents an hour, plus tips.

I started writing in English right away. At first, short poems. And I began to read in English with great voracity. I liked all the courses I was taking: two English classes (eleventh and twelfth grades), a speech class, American history, and gym. The first author I looked up in the school library was William Faulkner, of whom I had heard so much. But I found his English too dense for me at that point. Next I looked up Carson McCullers, who had been mentioned to me by a Colombian movie critic with whom I had corresponded. I read *The Heart Is a Lonely Hunter* and then all her books. But the book that really spoke to me was *Member of the Wed-*

ding. I identified with Jasmine/Frankie, the way I had identified with Jo in *A Taste of Honey*, with the added element that Frankie is gay.

In my speech class I memorized a monologue from Jean Anouilh's *Beckett*. Although no one understood a word I said, I recited the monologue with such emotion and passion that all my classmates burst into applause when I finished. Our teacher, Mrs. Susan Livingston, was really impressed and said that I could become a great actor if I wanted to. I had no desire to be an actor. I was a writer.

My English teacher in the eleventh grade (Mrs. Jacquie Bell) noticed that I was always reading. She began to take an interest in me, singling me out as the most insightful reader in the class. One day she was absent and a substitute came. Her name was Mrs. Choates, an old, elegant, imperious lady. We were discussing James A. Michener's autobiographical novel *The Fires of Spring*, the life of a young idealist who wants to be a writer. Suddenly, Mrs. Choates said to me, "Where are you going to college when you graduate?" Graduation, after all, was a couple of months away.

I had no idea and I said so. I had heard other kids mention going to college in the fall, but I thought that after high school I would get a job in Tampa so that I could live with my mother again. Tampa was at that time a small city with a large Latino population.

Mrs. Choates made a big fuss about me. She took me to see the principal and demanded he call Armando López, my guardian. Mrs. Choates wanted to know why a boy like me, who loved books and was very intelligent, had made no plans to go to college. Armando López said he was just a friend of my mother's, he was not in charge of my future. I had arrived too late in the school year to take the GED and too late to even get my picture in the yearbook.

One day Mrs. Livingston told the class that they didn't know how lucky they were, compared to me. Mrs. Jacquie Bell made me her pet. She made me promise that after I graduated I would keep in touch with her. She invited me to her home one day, and it was the first time that I envisioned a life for me in this country. She lived in an old, spacious southern house, and she had a grand piano and a collection of beautiful rocks she had dug out in the Midwest during her summer vacations. If I go to school, I told myself, and become a high school teacher, I too could live like this.

For graduation night I invited a classmate to be my date. She came to pick me up, it was raining, and on the way to the auditorium we had an accident. I don't think I ever even picked up my high school diploma.

By this time Mother had moved to Tampa, where she rented a room at an old couple's house. I was eager to join her. It meant we were one step closer to bringing my sister from Colombia so we could all live together again. The room we rented was in Ybor City, which historically had been the Latino section of Tampa. By the late sixties it was a slum, many of its fine old houses eaten away by termites. Now only poor Latinos—recent immigrants and blacks—lived in Ybor City. While I was attending Lakeland High, because of the fuss my teachers made over me, I didn't feel totally alone. But in Tampa I knew no one. My mother, with her wonderful social gifts, had already made a few friends. She found work sewing in a factory deep in the black section of Ybor City. Mother took me to the factory one Monday morning, and I applied for a job. I was hired to sort out the dirty linen that arrived from hospitals and restaurants. I would separate it in containers before it was sent away to be washed and pressed. We were the only Latinos working there. I hated my job. I hated every minute of it, standing all day long in garbage up to my ankles and breathing in the stench of rotten food.

I wrote to Mrs. Jacquie Bell to tell her about the new books I was reading: Orwell's *Animal Farm* and Huxley's *Brave New World*. She wrote back right away and pleaded with me not to let my mind go dormant, to make sure that somehow I made it to a junior college at least. A letter arrived from Mrs. Susan Livingston. It contained a check for $50, which she hoped I would use toward my college tuition. I went downtown with my mother to buy a suit. I thought that was a prerequisite for going to college.

I also wrote my first fan letter to a writer, to James Michener, whose *Fires of Spring* had moved me. A few days later I received a reply. Michener said that he wished me all the best and that he hoped someday he would read one of my published books. The letter was like a life jacket to a drowning man. On the way downtown to buy my suit the bus had passed by Tampa's public library. I made a mental note to go there on Saturday to see what books by Latin American authors I could find. In the letters my friend Josefina Folgoso wrote me from Colombia, she talked about a magnificent masterpiece, García Márquez's *One Hundred Years of Solitude,* and she mentioned the novels of an extraordinary generation of authors: Vargas Llosa, Donoso, Rulfo, Fuentes, Puig.

The Tampa Public Library at that time was housed in an old, dark building dating from the late 1800s. I spent all morning exploring the entire building. In a corner of the basement was a rack with books in Spanish. It was like finding a glorious treasure, the El Dorado I had searched for as a child. All the authors Josefina had mentioned were there in Spanish. But one book's title spoke to me instantaneously in a secret code. It was Manuel Puig's *Betrayed by Rita Hayworth.*

2

Manuel Puig
The Writer as Diva

The Argentinean expatriate writer Manuel Puig was one of the most effeminate men I've ever known. I met him in 1977 in a fiction workshop at Columbia University. The workshop was open to anyone in the city, and the only requirement was to submit a manuscript that Puig approved. I delivered my first novella to Puig at his Bedford Street address. Puig opened the door a tiny crack, took the manuscript, and asked me where I was from. When I said Colombia, he asked me a few questions about Cartagena. Then he promised to get in touch with me as soon as he read the manuscript. A couple of days later Puig called to say that I could attend the workshop, and he added that he liked my writing because it came "from under the epidermis." It would be nearly impossible for me to describe now how thrilled I was to hear this from an author I idolized with the complete and irrational ardor of youth.

I had read Puig's first novel, *Betrayed by Rita Hayworth,* in 1968 when I was barely out of high school and a new immigrant to the United States. This book, and the next two, *Heartbreak Tango* and *The Buenos Aires Affair,* with their mixture of movie lore, tangos and boleros, radical politics, Freudianism, and camp, spoke to me more directly than the work of any other Latin American novelist of "the boom." Puig became one of my cultural heroes of the 1960s. The headshot in the Spanish editions of his books published by Seix Barral showed him laughing, a mane of black hair swept back by the wind, and had given me a romantic crush on him. In that photograph he looked like an Italian movie star—a young but more refined Marcello Mastroianni.

Puig was in his midforties when I was his student. He no longer resembled the picture I had fallen in love with. The classical Mediterranean features were unchanged, but he was now a bit overweight, and his hairline had begun to recede. Although I had read some interviews with him, they didn't yield many clues about Manuel Puig the man. Toto, the boy-hero in *Betrayed by Rita Hayworth*, is daringly homosexual, and *The Buenos Aires Affair* has a homosexual subplot. So I assumed Puig's sexual orientation was gay—his camp sensibility certainly was.

In person he turned out to be more theatrical than Garbo: he had the same grand operatic gestures. Like Garbo's, his eyes were a tool, a weapon, organs not just for seeing but for expressing what he saw. Like the great diva, he raised his eyebrow (the left one) to indicate pain, disdain, despair. The eyebrow was a curtain raised or lowered to expose eyes alive with fire, eyes that could warm you or make you feel faint with their coldness. He had what in some circles are known as "Bette Davis eyes."

In those years I hadn't yet come out to my family or to many of my friends. Because in Colombian society there was only one kind of homosexual—*la loca* (the queen)—I had decided early on to cultivate a butch appearance. I grew a Ché Guevara beard, and I wore black leather jackets, jeans, and boots—the Christopher Street clone look of the time. I was determined not to be a stereotype of Latin culture. Puig, with his heightened drag queen mannerisms, aroused my worst fears; he represented everything in my adolescence I dreaded I would become. I did have a few effeminate friends back then, but I secretly felt ashamed to be seen with them in the heterosexual world. If I hadn't been obsessively drawn to Puig's novels, I might have been totally repelled by him. Some years later the painter Bill Sullivan told me that Puig, who was the first effeminate man he had ever respected, was a key figure in helping him face his own homophobia. Because opposites sometimes attract, a certain chemistry was immediately apparent between Puig and me. For a while, because of my macho act, he saw me as "a real man."

If he was openly homosexual in public, in private he was totally outrageous. He always referred to himself as "this woman," and he was merciless with closeted writers; quite perversely, he would refer to them as "she." He gave the names of movie stars to all the famous writers of the Latin American boom. In a remembrance of Puig, Guillermo Cabrera Infante wrote that Puig used to say of Carlos Fuentes that, like Ava Gardner "glamor surrounds her, but can she act?" Puig was subverting queeny bitchery, turning it into a valid instrument of critical discourse. This queeny affectation was in fact the heart of his art. He was saying that Fuentes was handsome, that he had a look, but that Fuentes is one of those luminaries admired more for the ambition he pours into his writing than for the writing itself. Puig used camp as a tool to get at the truth of things, as when he said of genre movies that they were treated in some countries "like women—to be enjoyed but not to be taken seriously." Or, when he declared, "Good taste can be a repressive force."

From the beginning I was aware that his ideas about homosexuality were more old-fashioned—and more radical—than mine. For example, he felt attracted exclusively to masculine types. He liked what in Latin culture is known as the *cacorro,* the *bugarrón,* the man who assumes the active role and who does not perceive himself as homosexual because he is usually married. This was the attitude of homosexuals who hired hustlers for sex twenty-five years ago. A hustler, back then, was by definition not a homosexual. What many gay men of the time wanted was the fantasy of going to bed with a straight man; they insisted that the hustler hold to the image of being straight. Hustlers were supposed to be straight; they did it just for the money. (For my generation those hustlers were not "real men" but closeted homosexuals.) In *Kiss of the Spider Woman,* which is essentially a Socratic dialogue, to the heterosexual Valentín's question, "And what's masculine in your terms?"—the queen Molina replies, "It's lots of things, but for me . . . well, the nicest thing about a man is just that, to be marvelous-looking, and strong, but without making any fuss about it, and also walking very tall."

Puig was too sane not to know the difference. He might have enjoyed his position exactly because it was so irrationally perverse. Later on, this exchange occurs between Valentín and Molina:

"And all homosexuals are that way?"

"No, there's the other kind who fall in love with one another. But as for my friends and myself, we're a hundred percent female. We don't go in for those little games—that's strictly for homos. We're normal women; we sleep with men."

"Sugar?"

"Please."

One night, after I had become Puig's friend, he spoke to me about a crucial moment when he was in his late twenties and realized he had done nothing with his life—except write farfetched, unmakable film scripts. He was talking to an old friend of his—"an old, divine queen"—who at that point told him, "Now you have two options: you can be a demented queen for the rest of your life, and spend all your time with hairdressers. Or you can become a real woman and turn all that queeny stuff into art." Puig paused—this was clearly the turning point of his life (that moment when all heroes hear the voice that reveals to them the nature of their quest). "That divine woman saved my life," he said. "If she hadn't told me that, I might have just been content with being a silly queen."

41

In the workshop at Columbia Puig made us rewrite other writers' stories. He told us that he wasn't interested in reading our autobiographies but that all writers need to learn structure, so he asked us to get inside the structure of finished works. The first assignment he suggested was the movie *Carrie,* and each of us chose a role (I was Piper Laurie, the mother), and we rewrote the story from the point of view of that character. I've come to think of him as a great teacher, not so much because of anything he did but because he made people who came in contact with him want to do their very best. The only consistent advice he gave me was, "Make it poetic."

Puig, who had just completed *Kiss of the Spider Woman,* encouraged me to write about gay themes. I started a homosexual novel, inspired by my first unhappy love affair. Later that fall I returned to the city with a completed manuscript. Puig read some of it and wasn't too enthusiastic (unwisely I had written it in English, thinking that in Spanish I would never find a publisher), but he urged me to publish *El cadáver de papá,* my first novella. That book had been rejected by many publishers in Spain, but with Puig's encouragement I sent it to the Institute of Colombian Culture, where it was accepted.

What had happened in the meantime was that I had become Puig's close friend, or, as he preferred to put it, one of his "daughters." He was not the first famous writer I met, but he was the first person I truly admired who took a keen interest in my fiction. In the winter of 1979 I introduced Manuel to a scientist friend, and we went out to dinner on a couple of occasions. Immediately, Manuel was fascinated by this man primarily because he was from Baghdad. Manuel was essentially someone who yearned to be seduced by the exotic and by romance. Growing up in General Villegas, a dusty hamlet in the pampas, he had yearned for greenery and glamor, and he actively sought both for the rest of his life. In the movies he loved, and in real life he had a great passion for the tropics. Creating a home in a tropical paradise became a major obsession.

In the spring of 1978 I returned to Bogotá, and later that year I received a letter from Manuel mentioning his desire to visit Colombia. In June 1979 I ran into him at a Writers' Congress in the Canary Islands. His *Pubis Angelical* had just come out, and Manuel was delighted that it was a best-seller in Spain. Those ten days in the Canary Islands we were inseparable, and Manuel introduced me to Severo Sarduy and other prominent novelists and critics from the Spanish-speaking world. I was a newcomer to that world, and he presented me as "my daughter, the debutante." Whereas a few years earlier I would have been offended by his feminization of me, he had had a liberating influence, freeing me from my robotic butch ideas and making me more relaxed about my sexuality. I learned that it was not only okay but also enjoyable to camp. When we parted, he announced his decision to visit Colombia a couple of months later.

I caught up with him again in Bogotá. It was then I realized how unhappy he was. Over many talks several things became clear: that he couldn't stand New York City anymore because of the failure of the love affair that he later transformed into the fiction of *Eternal Curse on the Reader of These Pages* and that he was crushed by how badly *Kiss of the Spider Woman* had been received by the critics. Robert Coover had panned it in the Sunday *New York Times*.

Puig had come to Colombia to attend a Writers' Congress in Cali, but after the congress ended, although he received and accepted invitations to visit other cities, he had no real reason to remain in the country. He claimed that it was good to visit different countries because it spurred the sales of his books. He was, he acknowledged, looking for a city in Latin America where he could settle down. He thought Cartagena might be it. Greta Garbo, Yoko Ono, and Joan Didion had all recently visited the resort.

In the late 1970s Puig was one of the most widely admired and read authors in Latin America, second only to García Márquez. Yet the reception he received in staid conservative Bogotá was less than an apotheosis. Because he wanted to go to Cartagena for a few weeks to explore the possibilities of living there, I introduced him to Gloria Zea, director of the Institute of Colombian Culture, who suggested a national homage to Manuel Puig. With the cooperation of the Instituto Colombo-Americano, a series of events was planned for his return. Cartagena, where García Márquez was to settle for a few years in the 1980s, did not work out for Puig. In a letter Manuel wrote me from Cartagena, he praises the beauty of the place but complains about the barrenness of its cultural life. The other piece of interesting information is that, despite feeling very lusty, he's working hard on *Eternal Curse on the Reader of These Pages* and that he hopes to complete its first draft soon.

Back in Bogotá, he gave talks at the Cinemateque, the Centro Venezolano de Cultura, and at the Centro Colombo-Americano; mobs of adoring fans came to see him. Bogotá's intellectuals, however, stayed away. Even his acquaintances (magazine and newspaper editors who had been supportive of his writing) and his publishers in the city weren't calling on him. When I started asking among my acquaintances why this was so, people used *Kiss of the Spider Woman* to mock Puig and to make disparaging remarks about him. It became obvious what was happening: the literary establishment could not forgive a major author of the "boom" for coming out with a gay novel. Many heterosexual and closeted writers (especially the latter) did not want to be associated with a well-known *loca*.

He was indeed a queen but also one of the most tough-minded people I've ever met. One morning during his stay in Bogotá, we had arranged to visit the colonial town of Villa de Leyva. Right before I left my apartment that morning to pick Manuel up at his hotel, I learned an acquaintance of mine had committed suicide. I went with the driver to the hotel and told Manuel what had happened and why it might be a good idea to postpone the trip until the following day. Manuel didn't like the idea at all. He said that my friend was dead and there was nothing I could do for him—why postpone for tomorrow what we could do today? He said that tomorrow, when I was feeling better, we'd go see something else. I was hurt and shocked but I went along with his plan. That day Manuel opened up to me in new ways. He talked about how he thought the British were the most racist people on earth; about how there was nothing he hated more than the Italian intellectual bourgeoisie; about how the most beautiful men in the world were in the countries behind the iron curtain. He didn't have a title for the novel he had completed in Cartagena. For an hour or so we played with hundreds of titles. Every new title he considered he would translate into English, French, Italian, Portuguese, and German, and if a title didn't sound inevitable in all those languages, he'd reject it immediately. Finally he arrived at *Eternal Curse on the Reader of These Pages*. I said that I would never buy a book with a title like that. He was so amused that he decided this was a good omen.

In the most delicate way possible I touched upon the reception he had been given by some of his Bogotá "friends"; I thought perhaps he wanted to let off steam. Very seriously, he said: "Remember what Don Quixote says to Sancho Panza: 'If the dogs are barking, it means we are riding.' " I was astonished he was quoting from a book, because he vehemently denied reading books. In fact, after I had known him for a while, I realized that he read voraciously—he just never kept copies of the books he read. At that point in his life this may have been because his place on Bedford Street was a cubbyhole—the smallest studio I've seen in New York.

Hanging out with him during those months in Colombia, I was struck by what a modest man he was. He thought wearing a tie was giving a bad example to people, and he dressed in clothes he might have bought in a secondhand store. Whenever we were invited to a beautiful home, he would pause before entering it and say: "Rich people's home!" as if somehow he felt he didn't belong there. He was fiercely proud of his lower-middle-class background. One day we were discussing an "aristocratic" writer we knew. Manuel said, "I'm so thankful I was born with the drive of a middle-class girl. Imagine having to get over all the hang-ups of those people." One of his favorite Mexican movies was the 1940s melodrama *Nosotros los pobres* (We the poor).

Manuel left Colombia, and later I went back to New York. That year, 1979, he sold the American paperback rights to four of his novels, and for the first time (amazing, considering he had been translated into fourteen languages and his books had sold hundreds of thousands of copies) he had a big lump of money to escape from New York, which he had come to hate. He moved down to Rio de Janeiro. But after the failure of *Kiss of the Spider Woman, Pubis Angelical* could not find a publisher in the United States, and when the bleak *Eternal Curse* came out it was dismissed as insignificant.

Fortunately, Rio de Janeiro worked for him. Manuel brought his mother to Rio, and they lived in apartments a block apart. Once he described his daily routine to me: in the mornings a swim with his mother, then several hours of writing, followed by lunch and a nap. A little more work in the afternoon, and he would spend the nights watching movies on tape with his mother and friends who came to visit. It sounded like an ideal existence. He had resumed his relationship with a married construction worker he had met many years before, "a real man," and they saw each other a couple of times a week. When he visited New York in the late '80s he looked younger and healthier than when I first met him. He had cultivated a Julio Yglesias tan, lost his baby fat, and even his hair had stopped falling out. He would strut his svelte figure. "Touch it," he'd say, "it's real woman's flesh."

Puig used to say that there are two kinds of books: those that die and those that live on. *Kiss* had been a flop with the intellectuals and the critics, but it turned out to be one of those books that lives on. From the beginning stage adaptations popped up all over the world, in some cases by writers and in some cases by actors. Filmmakers such as Fassbinder and Liliana Cavani wanted to turn it into a film. Manuel would throw a fit whenever he heard of a new stage production of *Kiss* done in Latin America or in Europe without his permission. He decided to put an end to this by adapting it himself. When his version was staged in Rio, it became a huge success.

He also wrote a novel in Portuguese, *Blood of Requited Love*, which was badly translated into English and reviewed with little sympathy; it was one of his least successful books. Reviewing the novel, I found it amorphous but stirring and lusty. It impressed me as a brave effort on his part to break out of his creative crisis. In a letter Manuel sent me from Rio, he expresses surprise at the poor reception the book received. He talks about how the novel was ignored and wonders whether it is because the protagonist is such a hot stud. He has read the script of *Spider Woman* and thinks it is bad. The Argentinean movie made of *Pubis Angelical* horrifies him. In a touching passage he talks about how *Spider Woman* has finally appeared in Argentina after being banned for many years. What Manuel cannot understand is why the book has been completely ignored in the Argentinean press, although hundreds of articles have appeared about it all over the world and the novel is required reading in the French university curriculum. He ends by saying that Argentina's total silence about this work is perhaps a sign of how terrified the country is of the complexities of the soul.

Perhaps disheartened by the reception his novels were getting during this period, he turned to playwriting. He wrote *Under a Mantle of Star,* a sex farce that verges on the fantastic and achieves moments of playful and wicked lyricism. Ronald Christ translated it with verve into English and published it with Lumen Books. It was staged in various countries where it failed. He wrote two other plays during these years, *Mystery of the Rose Bouquet* and *Golondrina Triste Macho.*

People began to talk about how Puig's career seemed to have gone into an irreversible decline. During that period survey articles on Latin American literature entirely ignored him or treated him as a minor writer.

All this changed, of course, in 1985 when Hector Babenco's movie version of *Kiss* opened to considerable commercial success and critical acclaim. Suddenly, at fifty-two Puig was hot again. In fact, he was more famous than he had ever been. *Pubis Angelical* found a publisher in English, and it even received a few good notices, which is not surprising, considering that it is a superb book. Mario Vargas Llosa began a review of a Brazilian novel in the Sunday *New York Times* by referring to Puig as one of the masters of contemporary Latin American fiction. All his books were reprinted again. For the first time in a long career he was financially secure. He was finally receiving the accolades he craved.

Although *Heartbreak Tango* and *Pubis Angelical* were made into films (Manuel was fond of some moments in *Heartbreak,* for which he had written the screenplay), neither was an international success. Perhaps whatever the quality of Babenco's version of *Kiss,* Puig should have been delighted with it because it restored his international reputation. Yet he hated it. Of William Hurt's celebrated performance, Manuel said, "*La* Hurt is so bad she probably will win an Oscar." She did. Babenco once told me he thought this was because Manuel could not conceive of anyone other than Manuel playing the role of Molina. To a certain extend Babenco is right. (Manuel did like some actors who played Molina on the stage.) With the exception of Toto—the star-struck boy in *Betrayed by Rita Hayworth*—there was more of Puig in Molina than in any of his other creations. Molina is what Toto might have grown up to be, if Manuel had not met the friend who urged him to turn his giddiness into art. In *Betrayed by Rita Hayworth* Toto fantasizes about Raúl García, the man he has a crush on. In the fantasy the two of them go to live in a cottage after Toto has fainted and García saves him from a bear. García revives Toto with hot beverages and sandwiches. To repay his beloved, Toto tells him a new movie every night. One game they play involves trying to decide which movie is the most beautiful of all. Toto, like Molina, makes up his own movies (set in the tropics, of course) in which Raúl García and Toto's favorite schoolteacher are involved in a torrid story that the Marlene Dietrich of *Seven Sinners* might have played in. Toto, like Molina, like Puig, is interested exclusively in tawdry, glitzy, escapist movies. He likes movies because of their exotic locales, glamorous settings, handsome leading men, marvelous gowns, and beautiful actresses, especially the ones who die at the end. Toto dislikes Myrna Loy because she never dies in any of her films.

It was fitting, then, that a movie adaptation of his work made Puig into one of the most celebrated authors of the world—because movies, not literature, were his first love. In an interview he gave me for the Colombian newspaper *El Tiempo*, he said the three main influences on his work were Greta Garbo, the films of Ernst Lubitsch (his early novels appear to be indebted to *The Shop Around the Corner*), and Freud. Actually, there was a typo in the newspaper and *Freud* came out as *Freed*. Manuel was delighted because he said that Arthur Freed, who produced the most demented of Busby Berkeley's musicals, was also one of his major influences. Puig had written dozens of screenplays before and after he became a novelist, and some were published in Spanish by Seix Barral. His adaptation of José Donoso's *Hell Has No Limits* was turned by Arturo Ripstein into a powerful, tenderly grotesque film. The opening selection of Joseph Papp's 1991 Latino Film Festival was Leonard Schrader's abominable *Naked Tango*, a movie "inspired" by an idea of Puig's. These lucrative movie jobs made him a rich man. At the end of his life his work entered the mainstream of Western consciousness. The popular Oscar-winning movie *Cinema Paradiso* has a boy hero named Toto who loves movies more than reality. It is an obvious homage to the main character of *Betrayed by Rita Hayworth*.

In the late '80s Puig came to New York to give readings and to receive honors. In 1987 Barnard College held a weeklong celebration of his work and I spent time with him on the last day. There was a reading of his theatrical adaptation of *Kiss* and afterward a long reception in which he was interviewed by journalists and photographed over and over. As I recall, hundreds of women wanted their picture taken with him. Some seemed to be generations of the same family of Latinas: grandmother, mother, and daughter. To each and every one he was obliging and kind. It wasn't just fag hags who adored him. (Although a lesbian friend of mine confessed she was offended by Manuel's impersonation of a woman because in her view what he had adopted was a stereotype of the vamp—an invention of patriarchy that perpetuates the image of woman as a frivolous sexual animal.) But many heterosexual women adored him personally and adored his work. In interview after interview he talked about how it was the masculine principle that was responsible for war and for destruction. He was an impassioned believer in the anima and believed that if everyone accepted it, we'd be more loving. And, of course, with a few variants (Valentín in *Kiss* and the macho hero of *Blood of Requited Love*) most of his characters are women and variations of Toto—of himself. Because he had spent his childhood and adolescence surrounded by women, listening to them, wanting to be one of them, waiting to become one of them, he understood how women are when they are with each other. *Betrayed by Rita Hayworth* and *Heartbreak Tango* have hundreds of pages of conversations of women talking about the detritus of their lives, the men they love, the oppression they feel at the hands of their insensitive husbands, their favorite movies and movie stars, the hairdos they like, the dishes they love to make. These banal subjects somehow become sublime in his empathetic rendering: in these conversations we hear our mothers, our aunts, ours sisters, the women we have loved. It is the same world that Flaubert satirized in *Madame Bovary*. No woman novelist would ever have thought of depicting women like Puig's for fear of being labeled superficial, lightweight. Feminists couldn't have done it either, because these characters defy all political agendas. Homosexuals usually do it in camp terms—women as bitches: funny monsters we can laugh at. Because Puig thought of himself as a woman—one of the women he grew up with—he wrote about them without a chip on his shoulder. If Vittorio De Sica had made, during his great neorealist period, a movie about women conversing—think of the maid in *Umberto D* talking to the grandmother in *Miracle in Milan*—the movie might have had some of the beautiful moments of being that Puig achieved in his first two novels. And because the Toto/Molina alter ego is a nonthreatening male and a victim, someone for whom we can feel sorry, it's no wonder women adopted Puig. When he ran into trouble, it was with the feminists, who accused *Pubis Angelical* of being self-pitying in its portrayal of a mad, wounded woman victim—which is how in some periods of his life Puig saw himself.

That night at Barnard he insisted that I stay until the end, and when it was over, we walked down Broadway, past Columbia where we had met, to a restaurant in the neighborhood. Along the way he was greeted by students who'd yell, "Hey, Manuel Puig!" Manuel purred, *"Viste qué famosa"* (See how famous she is).

He seemed very fulfilled. That night he talked about how he had never

really had a lover because "men don't like successful women." During dinner, for the first time ever, he bragged a bit about his acquaintances with
celebrities such as Madonna and Sonia Braga. That these glamorous sex
goddesses sought him out meant a lot to him. I teased him that the people
I met nowadays referred to him as a recluse, as if he were a Garboesque
figure. He gave me his Mona Lisa smile.

I saw him once more, in 1990, when he appeared at the 92nd Street Y.
He read that night from *Eternal Curse,* and he gave the lines a homosexual
and seductive subtext that was not clear on the printed page. The novel
struck me then as a kind of gay *Waiting for Godot.* Perhaps this novel, like
his other late work, was meant to be a play after all. The lines crackled
with sexual innuendo, pathos. The story was bleak all right, but it was also
funny, piercing; it worked beautifully on the stage. In the question-and-
answer period (the audience again was largely female), he talked about his
new novel, *Tropical Night Falling,* which was, he said, a book about how
old people need someone young to love.

Afterward there was a small reception, and he announced, to my surprise, he was to moving to Cuernavaca because the AIDS crisis had turned
Rio into a plague city.

Later in 1990 I was in touch with him because he had accepted an invitation to read at the PEN American Center Benefit for Writers and Editors
with AIDS. I mentioned to him that in the past few years I'd been teaching
Kiss of the Spider Woman and that I felt his presence close to me whenever I discussed the book. For many years I considered *Heartbreak Tango*
to be his masterpiece, but *Kiss* had begun to yield more profound layers
of meaning. I think it's one of the greatest love stories ever written, one of
the most daring and innovative novels of our century, and a work of mystical radiance. No other story so successfully combines the art of fiction
with the cinema. And of course I discovered why Manuel had quoted from
Don Quixote back in Bogotá: it is another reworking of Cervantes's opus.
In Puig's version both Molina and Valentín are each Quixote and Sancho
Panza. Like *Don Quixote, Kiss* is many books in one; it is an exploration of
the human need for freedom and fantasy and dreams to persevere and to
triumph even in the face of the greatest odds. It is a book about what a re-
demptive force love can be. The message of *Spider Woman* seems to be this:
Molina, the frivolous queen, begins, through his discussions with Valentín, to care about the misery of the world. Valentín (the unimaginative cold
Marxist) learns from Molina that we cannot divorce the mind from the
heart and that fantasy can be a liberating force. In the course of the novel
the two men enlarge their identities. Initially, Valentín is the Don Quixote
who wants to transform the world and Molina his Sancho Panza. At the

end Molina, by accepting political responsibilities, decides to go out in the world to help tilt at windmills. When Molina dies and Valentín is tortured, only his capacity for fantasy (which he has learned from Molina) keeps him alive. The two men merge; they become Siamese twins. Although in the beginning of the action they have little sympathy for each other, near the book's conclusion Molina admits, "And what scares me most is that they might separate us." These two alienated people begin to escape the isolation of the self, the loneliness of the human condition. At one point Valentín admits to feeling peaceful "maybe because I'm not thinking about me." A little later, Molina says,

"Just then, without thinking, I put my hand up to my face, trying to find the mole."

"What mole? . . . I have it, not you."

"Mmm, I know. But I put my hand to my forehead, to feel the mole that . . . I haven't got."

And later,

"It seemed as if I wasn't here at all . . . like it was you all alone. . . ."

Without waiting for Valentín to reply, Molina says, "Or like I wasn't me anymore. As if, somehow . . . I . . . were you." As he is dying, Valentín remembers and understands Molina's definition of love: "That I live deep inside your thoughts and so I'll always remain with you, you'll never be alone."

In Virginia in July 1990 I received the news of Manuel Puig's death in Cuernavaca. Although I knew I loved him, the depths of the grief surprised me. The suddenness of his death, coupled with its timing—he was beginning a new life—seemed like a heartless joke. The *New York Times* obituary was filled with bewildering information: it claimed his survivors, in addition to his mother, María Elena (Doña Male) de Puig, were a brother, Carlos Puig, and two sons, Javier Labrada and Agustín García Gil. The two "sons," were obviously two "daughters"—as he referred to several younger people he was close to. Nonetheless, gay writers who knew him were incensed that somehow the mention of two sons made him appear heterosexual to those who didn't know him.

Necrophilia is a strong impulse in Argentine society and in Latin culture, and soon after Puig's death an absurd mythology, a strange mythological web, began to grow as if he were a literary Evita Perón. In death he became an even more baffling figure than he was alive. Although he officially died of a heart attack brought about by a gall bladder operation, I began to hear stories that he had been ill with AIDS. Some people close to him reluctantly began to acknowledge it, whereas others denied it vehemently, as if having the disease would somehow make him a lesser man and tarnish his achievements. After all, if homosexuality is the greatest taboo in Hispanic culture, AIDS is the unspeakable. (Even many openly gay intellectuals have an attitude of denial toward the disease.) I couldn't help but think he would have liked all the confusion. Because, like Molina, Manuel always, always, always wanted to be a fabulous heroine.

That fall the grief over his death lingered. He had indeed been my literary mother, and I was grieving him as if my good mother had died. The bereavement was compounded because so many questions about his death were unresolved, and also because Reinaldo Arenas (the other major homosexual Latin writer and a friend and neighbor, who also insisted he knew firsthand that Manuel had died of AIDS complications) was himself dying of the disease.

I decided I would travel to Mexico to try to find out what had happened to Manuel.

I arrived in Mexico City on July 22, 1991. Only when I had been there a full week did I realize my arrival had coincided with the first anniversary of Manuel's death. The objective of my trip was to try to talk to Javier Labrada and Agustín García Gil, the "sons," and also to see the house where Manuel had died.

I had called Javier Labrada from New York to ask for an interview. I had his phone number and address because for a while Manuel had received his correspondence there while he was settling down in Cuernavaca. Javier Labrada agreed to meet me and asked me to call him upon arriving. I phoned him the day after I landed in Mexico City. Because he was out, I left messages for him both at home and at his office. While waiting for him to get in touch with me, I called my other acquaintances in the city and set out to do some sightseeing. When I mentioned the purpose of my trip to the intellectuals I met, I was told that the rumor in Mexico was that Manuel had had AIDS because no one had seen him during the eight months he had lived in Cuernavaca. Another theory was that he had died because he was so tight-fisted with his money that he had chosen not to go to a good hospital in Mexico City (I had heard this already). I was told how Manuel wasted three critical days during his illness calling hospitals in Mexico City inquiring about rates and that he had chosen to go to the clinic in Cuernavaca because it was the least expensive. The conventional wisdom was that no one in his right mind would have an operation in Cuernavaca. Three days after my arrival I called Javier Labrada again. He was in his office and he was very nice and queeny, and we made plans to meet on Saturday at the Café El Parnaso.

So on Saturday at 10:05 (he had insisted we meet at exactly five minutes past the hour) Javier Labrada, wearing a *Phantom of the Opera* t-shirt, walked to my table under the awning of the café. He was in his forties, but because he was a bit plump and had a pink complexion, there was something babyish about his face. His henna hair, with silver streaks, and his agate eyes are striking. It is a face that, because of its seeming innocence and vulnerability, draws you in to listening to him. After sitting down and ordering coffee, he began to narrate Manuel's last days. He talked, using his hands like darting butterflies around his head; sometimes it seemed he was playing the castanets. These were Manuel's mannerisms, the ones that William Hurt borrowed for his portrayal of Molina in *Kiss of the Spider Woman*. Labrada referred to Manuel always as Rita or "my mommy." For almost two and a half hours he spoke nonstop. Because I wanted him to feel at ease, I didn't take notes. Here is what I am able to remember of our conversation.

I asked him about the *Times* obituary in which he and Agustín García Gil had identified themselves as Puig's sons, and the confusion this had caused among those who knew Manuel. Labrada's deadpan explanation was, "Rita had two daughters: Yasmin (Agustín García Gil) and Rebecca (Becky), myself. I'm the daughter by Orson Welles and Yasmin is the daughter by the Aga Khan. I inherited Rita's brains and my father's figure." What had happened was that when the international news agencies began to call the family as soon as the news of the death broke, Labrada was asked repeatedly who he was, and he had thought the best way of taking care of it was to identify himself as a son. About Agustín García Gil—the other daughter—Labrada said that he lived in Monterrey. At one time they had been enemies. After Yasmin's visits Labrada would ask Puig, "Did you disinfect the house thoroughly?" However, at the end of Manuel's life they had reconciled and now they are good sisters once again. Labrada said that he took a lot of flack for identifying himself to the press as one of Puig's sons, that many people accused him of doing this because he wanted to keep Puig's fortune. The house in Cuernavaca had been in Labrada's name because, as a foreigner, Manuel could not own property in Mexico until his situation was legalized. "I could have crossed my arms and said nothing," Labrada said. "But I couldn't have done that to my mommy. I turned everything over to Rita's mother." I asked him then about Carlos, the brother who appeared suddenly like the evil twin sister in a Hollywood movie. Labrada had met him years before in Buenos Aires and winced when he spoke his name. Carlos, who was ten years younger than Manuel and never got along with him, became the executor of the estate. "But I won't say anymore," Labrada said. "My mommy wouldn't have wanted me to talk about this."

I asked him then, "Did Manuel have AIDS?" Labrada denied the rumors vehemently. He said that Manuel did not see anyone during his last eight months because he was getting the house ready to begin receiving friends and fans. If Manuel was thin, it was because he dieted and because he was an exercise freak. What's more, as the final details of the house were completed, Manuel had said, "Now the glamor begins."

He spoke at length about Manuel's plays: just a couple of weeks before my arrival *Mystery of the Rose Bouquet* (which Labrada produced) had closed down. He told me about his trip with Manuel to Hollywood for the premiere of this play starring Anne Bancroft and Jane Alexander. According to Labrada, le tout Hollywood had been in attendance: Sally Field, Daryl Hannah, Gena Rowlands. Bancroft had optioned the play for the movies. He also told me about their trip to New York City to see the final previews of the musical made of *Kiss of the Spider Woman*. Manuel had been very upset that the musical version apparently had failed. The *New York Times* had unfavorably reviewed a preview performance given outside New York, and plans for the Broadway opening were postponed indefinitely. However, the creative team kept developing the musical, and three years later, after Puig's death, it opened on Broadway to much acclaim, receiving seven Tonys, including best musical.

The subject turned to Manuel's Brazilian lovers: a young man and an older man—the married construction worker. Labrada characterized these relationships as "love in the shadows. She [Manuel] was the other one." A few weeks before he died, Manuel had received a postcard from the older lover, commemorating the twenty years of their first meeting. Manuel had been extremely touched by this romantic gesture.

He told me that Manuel was careful not to use the feminine in front of his mother but that sometimes the mother would use the feminine to refer to Manuel and Javier. And that sometimes, when Doña Male was watching a movie at home, Manuel would stand behind her, and unbeknown to her, would dance Rita Hayworth's "Put the Blame on Mame" number from *Gilda* as well as other famous numbers. Manuel had worked out a schedule for his mother, so that she watched one movie in the morning and one in the afternoon.

He told me that the Sunday night before Manuel died they had been watching John Ford's *The Lost Patrol* on video, which Manuel had disliked and had turned off. Two days later Manuel started complaining of pains and vomiting. His doctor was on vacation and Manuel got worse quickly. When another doctor finally arrived, he recommended that Manuel go to a hospital for surgery. Manuel chose to go to La Central Quirúrgica Las Palmas, a small private hospital in Cuernavaca. He came out of the operation delirious, and they had had to strap him down. Labrada became alarmed about Manuel's condition. To test Manuel's soundness of mind, Labrada asked him some questions about Alexander Korda's *The Private Life of Don Juan,* starring Douglas Fairbanks, Sr., and Merle Oberon, which was playing that night on Mexican television. When Manuel correctly answered all the questions about the plot, the actors, and details of the production, Labrada decided that he wasn't that ill. Little by little he improved, and two days before his death the doctors mentioned he would be leaving the hospital the following Tuesday. On Tuesday, shortly after midnight, Labrada received a phone call from the hospital informing him that Manuel had died. When he arrived at the hospital, he found Manuel covered with flowers that Doña Male had ordered for him.

"I can't forgive that woman for leaving me like that," Labrada said softly, wounded by the betrayal of this premature death. "I know that I will meet with her again in the next world because I have many questions for her."

"I do too," I said. I felt that Manuel's death was badly timed. After a period during which, for a variety of reasons, my life and my career had collapsed, only in the past few years had I begun to pick up the pieces, and I wanted Manuel to see me thriving and published again. Some months before I had sent him my short story "The Day Carmen Maura Kissed me," and I had been happy when he said that he loved it.

I asked Labrada how Manuel's death had been received in the Mexican press and in the country's intellectual circles. One paper, Labrada said, had published a picture of Manuel's coffin in the funeral parlor. The parlor had been closed to everyone, awaiting the family's arrival. The paper's headline proclaimed: "Puig dies alone!" "Rita wasn't alone," Javier Labrada said bitterly, "I was there with her all the time." He also spoke about a memorial service attended by many intellectuals and Argentine diplomats, the Argentine flag prominently displayed.

I mentioned what bothered me the most: had Manuel's ashes been returned to Argentina? After death threats were made when *The Buenos Aires Affair* was published, and later after *Kiss* was banned, he refused to return home. Considering how much he had made a point of staying away from his country, even when he lived for ten years next door in Brazil, I felt it would have mocked his wishes if, when it was no longer up to him, he had ended up returning. "My mommy and Doña Male were atheists," Javier said. "Mommy was cremated and I kept her ashes for seven months. The best way I can answer your question," he said, pausing and assuming an enigmatic pose borrowed from Manuel, "is to say that I've smoked many cigars in my life . . . perhaps what returned to Argentina were my cigar ashes . . . perhaps Mommy's ashes were scattered by me all along Orquídea Street which she loved so much." "So the ashes that returned to Argentina were anything but Manuel's?" I asked, laughing aloud. "I leave you with that doubt," Labrada said, putting on a naughty-boy expression.

Javier Labrada programs the movies for Mexican national television, and it's because of this connection that the relationship began when Manuel arrived in Mexico in 1974 to do research for the Mexican movie that appears in *Kiss of the Spider Woman*. It's obvious that Labrada adored Manuel, that he was his greatest fan. To Javier, Manuel was a superstar diva. Before we parted I asked Labrada for Manuel's last address in Cuernavaca. He gave it to me and offered to call the man in charge of the grounds so that I could see the house.

The following morning the friend at whose house I was staying offered to drive me to Cuernavaca, which is an hour away from Mexico City and is situated in a small green valley hugged by rolling hills. It is a town where many well-off people from the capital own weekend places. Also, hundreds of American retirees live there, as well as many famous people who go there to play tennis, swim in their pools, and bask in the sun. Among them are García Márquez, Carlos Fuentes, the Mexican movie diva María Félix, and other local and international celebrities. The late John Huston and Helen Hayes also owned property there. Cuernavaca's main asset is its perfect springlike climate, free from the pollution of Mexico City. Because it is closer to sea level, it has lush festive vegetation that mirrors the colorfulness of Mexican costumes and crafts. Manuel had told me that it was mainly for its "delicious climate" that he had decided to settle there.

The city has narrow winding streets that rise and dip; many of its parks, plazas, and boulevards are overgrown with vegetation. All the great houses are hidden by tall walls that sometimes are painted in a single arresting color that seems to have been dreamed up by the elegantly visionary architect Luis Barragán. Over these walls clusters of red, white, orange, and purple bougainvillea spill into the street.

It was 1 P.M. when we arrived at 210 Orquídea Street and rang the bell. We remained there for at least ten minutes, knocking on the wide black metal door and yelling, but there was no response. The only thing I could see from the street was the top of the satellite dish. We were back in the car, the engine running, when a boy opened the heavy metal door. In my nervousness I babbled a long speech about how I had been Manuel's student and had come all the way from New York to see the house. The boy, who must have been ten, seemed bewildered but invited us in. It was much later that it dawned on me that because the house was for sale, they would have shown it to me anyway.

Although I had imagined the house to be beautiful, the place was more magnificent than anything I could have ever imagined. It's a compound on four descending levels. The main house is on the right as you enter. It's a modern structure, largely of glass, built perhaps thirty years ago. Behind the house are extensive gardens and in front of it a bed of hundreds of white gardenias in bloom and dwarf magnolia trees. From this level one can see the hazy-blue mountains of the valley in which Cuernavaca sits. We didn't enter the main structure but kept on walking. I noticed the profusion of fruit trees and the hedges that separated this level from the next. Braided in on top of the hedges were long strands of a fiery red hibiscus called *llama-rada*—flames. My friend remarked that the hedges were regal looking, like those in the movie *Dangerous Liaisons*. As we kept descending, on our left was a garden of avocado, guava, orange, plum, and tangerine trees, as well as many other fruit trees unknown to me, one of them called *nacho*. Behind these trees, which were boxed by walls of multicolored bougainvillea, was a two-floor structure to which the boy referred as "the bungalow." Javier Labrada had told me that Manuel had not finished furnishing the top floor, which was to be the guest house. It consisted of a large living room, spacious kitchen, and two bedrooms, each with its own bathroom.

We left this house and took a staircase that led to Manuel's studio on the first floor, which contained tall glass windows and was the size of a Soho loft. It was especially striking because of its large lilac tiles. What I noticed first were the mounted posters leaning against the walls—a big poster of the Argentine movie version of *Heartbreak Tango* and posters of the theatrical productions of *Kiss of the Spider Woman* in German, Italian, Portuguese, Spanish, and French. Although sixteen boxes of books and documents had been shipped to an American university just a few days before, remnants of Manuel's library were visible in the twelve tall metal bookcases, one of which contained hundreds of volumes of Manuel's works translated into at least a dozen languages. Two piles of small telephone notebooks, marked "Diary," caught my attention. I looked through several of them, and they contained almost exclusively a detailed account of the movies he saw each day, the letters received, and so forth. Many of these little books spanned the years he had lived in New York. Opening one at random, I saw that for January 10, 1976, he listed: *They Drive by Night, A Date with Judy, Nancy Goes to Rio*. The following day, a Sunday, he listed *If I had a Million, The Falcon in Hollywood,* the Stephen Sondheim musical *Pacific Overtures,* and something called *Novak's Bondage*. Most days he listed three or four entertainments.

I was still looking through the books when the boy's father, the groundskeeper, came in. Adán Mendiolo García was a man in his early forties, with a surfer's deep tan, a black mustache, and handsome features. He was dressed in a white t-shirt, a red baseball cap, faded jeans, and sneakers. He said he was now taking care of the house until it was sold but that he had been Manuel's chauffeur-gardener and had lived on the premises with his wife—who did the cleaning of the compound—and their children.

I was feeling very moved by the books and posters, the beauty of the room into which sheets of light poured, and the size of this studio, which was at least ten times larger than the tiny hole-in-the-wall where Manuel had lived on Bedford Street. I felt a jabbing pain in my heart when Don Adán informed me that Manuel had died four days after completing the final details for the studio.

Leaving the room, we saw below us, on a meadow of lime-colored grass, a large purple pool whose water caught sunlight ripples. Manuel and his mother had been daily swimmers for many years. Don Adán said that a tennis court had been there originally, but Manuel had removed it to build the pool. "He didn't swim in it more than ten times," Don Adán sighed. The pool, of a surreal beauty, was like a huge David Hockney painting. To the right of the pool, on the last level, was another house where Don Adán and his family lived.

We took a path leading to the other side of the house and up into the gardens. Each level was decorated with geometric topiaries, more fruit trees (many bearing fruit), and beds of carefully arranged plants and flowering bushes. Don Adán explained that Manuel had planted most of the small plants and fruit trees and all the flowers.

We arrived at the first level, where Manuel and his mother had lived. The first room we entered was Doña Male's room. Next we entered the movie room, which also served as Manuel's studio while the other space was being remodeled. It still contained a gigantic dark shelf made of tree trunks where the TV and VCR rested. Then we walked down a hall that led to the other end of the house. On a lower level was a guest room that Don Adán described as "Don Javier's room." Its closet, some ten feet tall, had been crammed to the top with Manuel's thousands of movie tapes, Don Adán explained. Behind this room was the kitchen, which Manuel remodeled in a delicate light-colored wood. I was standing there taking in the beauty of the space when a huge spider emerged from the kitchen sink. I screamed, "The spider woman!" Don Adán laughed appreciatively. Next we visited Manuel's bedroom, which also had a private bathroom. Directly in front of the bedroom was a large room with a fireplace and huge windows: this served as living and dining room. The entire place, according to Javier Labrada, had been decorated with art nouveau antiques, and the curtains were a color that Manuel had described as Austrian melon. I closed my eyes and tried to picture this completely bare space decorated with the objects that Manuel had collected in the last decade of his life and with curtains from an MGM technicolor musical or an Ernst Lubitsch Vienna fantasy.

My friend and Don Adán's family wandered out of the room, but I sat on a chair near the wall next to a small telephone stand with at least a dozen letters from all over the world addressed to María Elena de Puig. Several statements from a local bank were addressed to Manuel.

Don Adán asked me then how well I had known Manuel. I told him about how I had been his student and then his friend for fifteen years and how the suddenness of his death had devastated me, and that was why I had traveled from New York, to try to answer all the questions in my head. Don Adán smiled. "You don't know how many journalists came here after his death trying to snoop, but I refused to talk to them," he said. "I wouldn't do anything to harm Don Manuel or the family. Don Manuel was such a good man. I wouldn't have changed him for a pile of money."

I realized that now, a year later, Don Adán wanted to discharge himself of his memories and his feelings for Manuel.

At first his memories had the startling oddity of thoughts that pop into our heads from nowhere. He talked about how he would drive Manuel into town to go to the bank. "Don Manuel would wear these old sandals and I would say, 'Don Manuel you can't go into town like that. You have to put on a pair of good shoes.' And he would say, 'But I have no good shoes.' He would take lots of money out of the bank in a brown paper bag, an old, tattered, dirty bag," he said smiling, "and we'd go shopping. Then on the way home I would ask him for the bag and he would say, 'I have no idea where it is.' We'd have to return to the last place where he had been, and of course it would be there. Who would ever think of taking such an ugly bag!" He paused, becoming thoughtful. "It's funny how sometimes we predict our own death," Don Adán said. "A couple of months before he died, he said to me one day in the car, 'You are the right person to take care of Mother after I'm gone.' 'Now what kind of thing is that to say, Don Manuel?' I said. 'You are the person who's going to take care of your mother. Why are you talking like that?' "

It seemed clear this man had loved Manuel and that Manuel had appreciated the gift of his presence in the last eight months of his life. When I think of Manuel, the first image I conjure up is his gentle thoughtful nature. Probably many people who loved him, as this man obviously had, possessed some of these same qualities. Don Adán talked eagerly about an event that had changed his life and the life of his family and that, a year later, still haunted him. His version contradicted much of what Labrada had told me. At first his tone had a deep sadness as he described, with a storyteller's attention to important details, the events that led to Manuel's death. On Monday, July 16, Manuel began having pains, chills, vomiting, and diarrhea. Manuel drank tea and refused to do anything about it. The following day he was much worse but didn't call anyone because his regular doctor in Cuernavaca was on vacation. By Wednesday his condition had deteriorated so much that a doctor was called. After a brief examination the doctor recommended that Manuel be taken to a hospital right away. It was then that Manuel decided to go to Central Quirúrgica Las Palmas. Manuel was so weak at this point that Don Adán had to carry him to the car. X-rays revealed that Manuel's gallbladder needed to be removed; the operation was performed. The first signs that something was amiss became apparent when the anaesthesia wore off. Manuel was delirious and very agitated. He started acting irrationally and pulled the IVs from his arms. "He just became afraid," says Don Adán. Because he wouldn't remain still, it was decided to strap him down to the bed. Don Adán asked for special bandages so they wouldn't cut his wrists, and Manuel was secured to the bed.

His condition began to deteriorate. Javier Labrada came to visit, and Male de Puig and Don Adán were by Manuel's side all the time. The following day the doctors called Don Adán outside the room and asked him if Manuel was a homosexual. Don Adán became irate. "You know how Don Manuel was," he said to me. "I was furious. I couldn't believe their lack of delicacy. I said that I had never seen anything untoward, and what did it matter anyway?" It was then that I pressed him: "Did they ask you if he was homosexual because they told you Manuel had AIDS?" Don Adán slumped against the wall, his face sank in his chest; staring at the floor, he remained silent. He seemed so shaken that I couldn't ask any more questions. After a while, with his head lowered, but his tone changing now to searing anger, he exploded: "The owner of the hospital was very bad to Don Manuel. The things I could say if I wanted to talk. But what for? Don Manuel had great difficulty breathing, his mouth was open all the time. I would give him drops of water and try to close his mouth. His tongue began to stick out: it was very dry, and then it turned green. I begged them to open his throat so he could breathe. . . . I was outside his room at 3:30 A.M. on Tuesday, when the doctor called me. He said, 'Did you know Manuel Puig?' I nodded. 'He's dead,' the doctor said. I went in. He was in bed, with his eyes wide open, staring at the lamp above his bed. He looked as if he had been spooked at the last moment. I closed his eyes."

According to Don Adán, Doña Male de Puig accepted Manuel's death calmly. I thought: almost as if she had been expecting it. We chatted for a while longer and then stepped out into the luminous afternoon. The smell of the gardenias was inebriating and I commented on it. "At night, when they all open up, there is such a sweet smell all over the house. Sometimes I walk through the rooms late at night, when everything is quiet, and I think about when Don Manuel and his mother were here, and I become so nostalgic," he reflected.

Although I was feeling sad, we drove directly to the Central Quirúrgica Las Palmas where I introduced myself to the nurse in charge at the main desk. She said that neither the doctors nor the nurses who had attended Manuel were in. I asked if I could see some of the hospital, and she told me to go ahead and look. Even by the standards of a developing country, the place was incredibly shabby. Some construction was going on, but the rooms were exceptionally tiny, dark, almost dingy, and it made me uncomfortable just looking at them. I couldn't help but feel that Manuel had chosen this place because he was trying to hide something.

We returned to Mexico City late in the afternoon. That night my head was full of questions. It was hard to believe that if Manuel had been ill with AIDS, and knew he was going to die, that he would have spent the last part of his life—all his energy—creating that dream house, when he must have sensed he would not live long enough to enjoy it. On the other hand, he may have denied his disease to himself. After all, terminally ill people sometimes undertake heroic enterprises—it becomes the fuel that keeps them going. They can also become obsessive collectors; the collections they leave behind become monuments to their taste.

The next day I woke up ready to return to Cuernavaca to talk to the doctors. And yet, as the morning wore on, I dithered. By noon I knew that I wasn't going to make the trip to Cuernavaca that day. I felt that perhaps Manuel didn't want me to go any further—that if he had tried so desperately to protect his privacy, I should respect his wishes. Garbo is reported to have said, "I don't care if I die, if Garbo lives." Puig, the control freak who devised a rigorous schedule of movies for his mother and for himself, had obviously wanted to orchestrate the final chapter of his life. Like Garbo, he wanted to be remembered as healthy, slim, youthful, and handsome. The parallels of his life with Garbo's *A Woman of Affairs* became singularly striking. Diana Merrick (Garbo) is, when the movie begins, a beautiful sunny girl untouched by life's sadnesses. But, impatient and reckless, Diana betrays Neville Holderness, the man she loves, and marries David Furness, who commits suicide on their honeymoon. Diana's reputation is tarnished and she's ostracized from London society. In the next few years she travels to Biarritz, Cairo, Monte Carlo, London, Paris, Nice, St. Moritz—a déclassé woman. A smug Londoner remarks, "One doesn't know her these days." However, to the bride of Neville Holderness, Diana is a "fascinating woman." At the end Diana dies, delirious, clutching roses to her chest in a gloomy hospital.

This scenario is not that different from the main outlines of Puig's life: just as suffering transforms Diana from a superficial girl into a fascinating woman, becoming a novelist and going through the ups and downs of a long career turned the giddy queen of Puig's youth into a person of weight, a great artist. Garbo could be enthralling when she was laughing and gay, but it was in her scenes of suffering, in *Camille,* for example, that she turned her acting into alchemy, into a practice of spiritual purity and incandescence. Like Garbo, Puig knew just when to withdraw, when to let the legend metamorphosize into myth.

The next day I left for Oaxaca. My first night there I began reading *Mystery of the Rose Bouquet.* I knew nothing about the subject matter of this play, written in 1986 and first performed in English in England in 1987. I must confess it surprised me (but not that much) that it is about a sick woman who's obsessed with death. The action takes place entirely in "an exclusive clinic," and the only other character is a nurse who is hired to somehow cajole the patient into eating. *Mystery* doesn't strike me as one of Puig's triumphs. *Under a Mantle of Stars* seems to me to be a fresher and livelier dramatic piece. *Mystery* isn't exactly empty, but there wasn't much to hold my attention, except perhaps when it seemed to shed light on Puig's life. Ultimately, the play has little to say, it's not very forceful, and it lacks conviction in the moments that it crosses from the real into the fantastic or magical. The play is saved from total failure by moments of sly and exquisite humor that sneak in once in a while. In the last moments of the piece *Mystery* takes an unexpected turn that is quite inspired, shining with Puig's wizardry. It also becomes quite beautiful and affecting. But for me, the last few lines—the patient's last lines—took on a poignant meaning that was quite impossible to ignore: "Tonight you have to decide your destiny. (*With humor*) To serve science, or love. Will it be the bustling activity of the hospital ward or the waiting in a garden, languishing, sunset after sunset . . . (*Pause.*) Making yourself dizzy with the scent of jasmine."

Reading these words, I could almost smell the four hundred bushes of gardenias that Manuel had planted in his house in Cuernavaca across from the living room. And I remembered Don Adán's words: "It's funny how sometimes we predict our own death." Then I thought: in the last eight months of his life Manuel had not written a line because he had been too busy building his first and last home in this world.

3

The Last Days
of Reinaldo Arenas
A Sadness as Deep
as the Sea

Early in December 1990 the literary agent Thomas Colchie called to say that the exiled Cuban writer Reinaldo Arenas—who lived around the corner from me, in Hell's Kitchen—was in what looked like the final stages of AIDS and that he had expressed a desire to hear from me.

I told Tom that I'd be happy to call on Reinaldo Arenas. I had known for some time that he was sick, but I had respected his decision not to discuss his illness with me. However, that year it became increasingly more difficult for me to run into him at the post office or the supermarket and to pretend that I didn't notice his emaciation and the Kaposi's sarcoma lesions that now gashed his visage. Although Reinaldo applied makeup to the spots on his face, I found it more disturbing to imagine what the lesions looked like than to see them.

I had met Reinaldo Arenas in 1981, when he arrived in New York from Miami after he left Cuba during what became known as the Mariel exodus to Florida. Colchie introduced us. I was thirty then, had returned to New York to settle down after a decade in which I commuted from Colombia to the States. I was then under contract with an American publisher to write a novel. Because I had an American lover, the painter Bill Sullivan, and because I had been educated in this country and felt myself part of New York's art world and writing scene, the differences between Reinaldo and me were huge.

Although he was an internationally known writer, he had lived in Cuba all his life. His parents were peasants, and he grew up as one. He was immensely well read and spoke other languages, but he didn't try to disguise his Goajiro origins. His teeth were crooked and full of cavities, and some were missing. He hadn't yet acquired, as most writers transplanted to New York eventually do, a sense of fashion and slickness. So Reinaldo didn't cut a glittering figure in the image-conscious gay scene. But my mother's family was a peasant family, and I spent time during my formative years living in the countryside, so I felt comfortable with him. Conversely, he must have sensed that I had managed to create an image of myself that was full of artifice and this probably amused him. That we were both openly homosexual Latin American writers was a bond much stronger than all the outward differences.

Something else brought us together: unlike most Latin American authors, I had never been a member of the leftist intelligentsia. When I was an adolescent in Colombia in the 1960s, it was unthinkable for a young intellectual to be unsympathetic to the Cuban Revolution and to the forces that advocated radical changes in countries like Colombia, semifeudal states run with an iron hand by a small group of despotic families. But in 1966 my mother, sister, and I emigrated to Florida. For the first time I came in contact with the Cuban refugees who had fled the island: those who Fidel Castro, and leftists all over the world, labeled *gusanos*—worms. I was torn in my allegiance toward the Cubans I met. On the one hand, many of them provided for us (we settled in Tampa, where few Colombians were living) the vast amount of support that recent immigrants need in order to survive in their new home. Still, I despised their values. They defended American policy in Vietnam, saw John F. Kennedy and the Democrats as communist sympathizers, and, because of their business ingenuity, placed undue emphasis on material success. They were openly racist. A large number of these south Florida Cubans were reactionary, and I, as a sympathizer with the humanistic ideals of socialism, felt alienated by their politics. Yet I was bewitched by their personal warmth, gift for laughter, gaiety, and open and giving nature when they bestowed their friendship upon you. I loved many of them as human beings, although I abhorred them as political symbols.

When Reinaldo Arenas arrived in New York in 1981, I was older, less dogmatic, more understanding of peoples' shortcomings. Also, I had had had ample opportunities to become disenchanted with the Stalinist Latin American left. Besides, it was clear that Fidel Castro was no friend of homosexuals—he had persecuted, tortured, and killed many. Cuba no longer appeared to me as an island of hope for a new and more just Latin America. Instead, it seemed an island-jail where noncomformity was punished and where human rights violations were common.

Thus it was with mixed feelings that I entered my friendship with

Reinaldo Arenas. Soon after Arenas's arrival my friend, the poet Tim Dlugos, asked me if I could arrange a meeting between the two of them. Tim wanted to interview Reinaldo for *Christopher Street* magazine. Reinaldo agreed to meet him at my apartment. On the appointed day Tim showed up with a tape recorder, and we sat around having drinks and a chat while we waited for Reinaldo. When he was a half hour late, I called to remind him, but there was no answer. Reinaldo had already devised a system for reaching him by phone: you called, waited for the phone to ring three times, and hung up. You called back right away, and then he knew it was someone he wanted to talk to and would pick up. At first I dismissed this and other peculiarities of his social behavior as Latin American eccentricities. I was reminded, for example, of heterosexual poet friends who never answered the phone themselves—the women in their households did. Much later, when I understood Reinaldo better, I realized his behavior was just an extension of the paranoia that exists in the Cuban émigré world. In Castro's Cuba dissidents had to devise elaborate systems of communication to avoid being spied upon; they had transplanted those attitudes to this country, as if here too they felt constantly under surveillance.

Tim Dlugos and I were hurt and disappointed that Reinaldo stood us up. Nonetheless, I made up my mind not to let this incident sour our incipient friendship. Reinaldo gave his first reading in Manhattan in a bookstore in the Village. He read in Spanish, and then his translator read in English. Reinaldo was a dramatic reader: he used his hands expressively and lowered and raised the volume of his voice to underscore key passages. At one startling moment in the reading he boomed a few sentences, letting each word hammer the air like an exclamation point. Before performance art became fashionable, he was doing it.

One memorable evening in 1981 the noted Cuban writer Severo Sarduy called me. (Sarduy died of AIDS several years later.) Because Sarduy lived in Paris, where he was the Latin American editor at Seuil Éditions, I assumed he was the person responsible for bringing Reinaldo's books out in French while Reinaldo was a prisoner in Cuba and his books had to be smuggled out of the country. Sarduy suggested we meet at a Cuban-Chinese restaurant on Eighth Avenue and 50th Street. He had never met Reinaldo. That night my lover and I went with Reinaldo to the restaurant to meet Severo and his French lover. For me it was an exciting moment, two prominent homosexual Cuban writers, who already had an important literary relationship, meeting for the first time. Yet the dinner was anticlimactic: Reinaldo was formal, almost stiff, betraying no emotions. I was disappointed. When the awkward meal was over, we returned to my apartment for drinks and talk. Later that night we went to the now defunct Haymarket, a notorious hustlers' bar on Eighth Avenue and 46th Street. Even there I felt that Reinaldo treated Sarduy strictly as a business acquaintance.

In 1983 my novel *Colombian Gold* was published, and it was met by mostly hostile reviews. Reinaldo's fortunes, on the other hand, rose. He received a Guggenheim Fellowship, and a Cintas Fellowship, which is given to distinguished Cuban artists. His epic poem *El Central* and the novels *Farewell to the Sea* (which Castro's police had destroyed in manuscript a few times) and *Old Rosa* appeared in English. Several other titles came out in Spanish and in many other languages. Reinaldo acquired a set of beautiful new teeth, started working out, and developed an impressive armor of well-defined muscles. With his movie-star smile his handsomeness was irresistible. After a lifetime of persecution and misery, in which he was jailed and witnessed suicides, rapes, cold-blooded murders, and torture, Reinaldo was enjoying success. I was, of course, jealous, but it was hard to resent him because we kept running into each other at the post office and the supermarket and he was unwaveringly friendly and kind. He encouraged me to apply for a Guggenheim and asked me to submit poems to *Mariel,* the Spanish magazine he edited during those years. Yet we stopped hanging out together, and our friendship now had a cautious edge. His all-consuming hatred of Fidel Castro—and of García Márquez for supporting the Cuban Revolution—combined with the searing intensity of his passions, terrified me. He could be nurturing, but there was, I learned, a truly Dostoyevskian side to his nature. Edmundo Desnoes, author of the celebrated novel *Memories of Underdevelopment* and a supporter of the Cuban Revolution, gave a talk at New York University to an almost exclusively leftist audience. Reinaldo attended and, incensed by Desnoes's favorable report of the revolution, called him a lying s.o.b. A fracas ensued: Reinaldo was thrown in the air and later pinned against a wall where he was hit by some men in the audience. Desnoes was unable to finish his talk. The Latino intellectual community was appalled and from that time on treated Reinaldo as an outcast.

By the mideighties so many of my friends had died of AIDS that I wasn't surprised when I realized Reinaldo was ill. His sexual appetite was voracious. Coming home late at night I would see him prowling Times Square or walking out of the sleaziest sex joints.

Reinaldo lived on 44th Street between 8th and 9th Avenues. He had visited my apartment many times yet had never invited me into his home. So when Thomas Colchie phoned in December 1990 and asked me to check on Reinaldo, I thought I'd better get in touch with him right away. Too many friends had died before we had a chance to say things we wanted to say. I called him, and we made plans for me to stop by late that afternoon.

I climbed the steps of Reinaldo's building and rang his buzzer. The building was a walk-up, and Reinaldo's apartment was on the top floor, the sixth. At the top of the steep stairs I knocked on his door. I heard what sounded like a long fumbling with locks and chains, which even in Times Square seemed excessive. The door opened, and I almost gasped. Reinaldo's attractive features were hideously deformed: half his face looked swollen, purple, almost charred, as if it were about to fall off. He was in pajamas and slippers. I can't remember whether we shook hands or not or what we said at that moment. All I remember is that, once I was inside the apartment, he started putting on the chains and locks, as if he were afraid someone was going to break down the door.

We went through the kitchen into a small living room. Besides an old-fashioned sound system and a television set, I remember a primitive painting of the Cuban countryside. A table, two chairs, and a worn-out sofa completed the decor. Reinaldo sat on the sofa and I took a chair. I felt that if I sat too close to him, I would not be able to look him in the eye. Stacks of manuscripts lay on the table—thousands and thousands of sheets, and Reinaldo seemed like a shipwreck disappearing in a sea of paper. When I asked if they were copies of a manuscript he had just finished, he informed me that the three manuscripts on the table were a novel, a book of poems, and his autobiography, *Before Night Falls.*

Reinaldo spoke with enormous difficulty, his voice a frail rasp. "The novel, *El color del verano,* concludes my Pentagony. It's an irreverent book that makes fun of everything," he mused. "*Leprosorio* is a volume of poems. And *Antes que anochezca,*" he pointed to the third pile, "is my autobiography. I dictated it into a tape recorder and an amanuensis transcribed it. It's going to make a lot of people mad."

It seemed to me absolutely protean the amount of writing he had managed to do, considering what a debilitating disease AIDS is. I said so.

"Writing those books kept me alive," he whispered. "Especially the autobiography. I didn't want to die until I had put the final touches. It's my revenge." He explained, "I have a sarcoma in my throat. It makes it hard for me to swallow solid foods or to speak. It's very painful."

"Then maybe you shouldn't talk. I'll do the talking," I offered, moving to the sofa.

"But I want to talk," he said curtly. "I need to talk."

I said, "Reinaldo, if there is anything you need, please don't hesitate to let me know. Whatever it is . . . cooking your meals, getting your medicines, going with you to the doctor, anything." I mentioned that the PEN American Center had a fund for writers and editors with AIDS and offered to contact them.

"Thanks so much, *cariño*," he said in the plaintive singsong in which he spoke. It was a sweet, caressing tone: melodious like a lazy samba but also mournful, weary, accepting of the hardships of life. This was a typically peasant trait. "There is a woman who comes to help three days a week. She does all my errands. Besides, Lázaro [Lázaro Carriles, his ex-lover who had remained his closest friend] comes by every day."

Just in case he wasn't aware, I mentioned other sources where he could go for help.

He snapped, "I don't like those men who serve as volunteers. I can't stand all that humility."

From where I sat I could see a bleached wintry sunset over the Hudson.

"But if you contact the PEN Club that would be good," he conceded. "I would like to get away from here before winter comes. My dream is to go to Puerto Rico and get a place at the beach so I can die by the sea."

To encourage him I said, "Perhaps your health will improve. People sometimes . . ."

"Jaime," he cut me off, "I want to die. I don't want my health to improve . . . and then deteriorate again. I've been through too many hospitalizations already. After I was diagnosed with PCP [AIDS pneumonia], I asked Saint Virgilio Piñera," he said, referring to the deceased homosexual Cuban writer, "to give me three years to live so that I could complete my body of work." Reinaldo smiled, and his monstrous face showed some of his former handsomeness. "Saint Virgilio granted me my request. I'm happy. I do wish, though, that I had lived to see Fidel kicked out of Cuba, but I guess it won't happen during my lifetime. Soon, I hope, his tyranny will end. I feel certain of that."

I knew better than to disagree with him when it came to discussing Fidel Castro. Once, in the mideighties, I had tried to tell him to put behind him his years of imprisonment and persecution, to forget Cuba, to accept this country as his new home and to live in the present. "You just don't understand, do you?" he had shouted, shaking with anger. "I feel like one of those Jews who were branded with a number by the Nazis; like a concentration camp survivor. There is no way on earth I can forget what I went through. It's my duty to remember. This," he roared, hitting his chest, "will not be over until Castro is dead. Or I am dead."

We talked for a while about the collapse of the communist states. The last thing I wanted was to upset him in any way, yet I had to defend my belief in socialism as the most humanistic form of government. So I spoke to that effect.

"On paper socialism is the ideal form of government," he said, not altogether surprising me. "It's just that it's never worked anywhere. Perhaps some day." Becoming thoughtful, almost as if talking to himself, he added, "Jaime, what a life I've had. Even before the revolution, it was bad enough the agony of being an intellectual queen in Cuba. What a sad and hypocritical world that was," he paused. "Finally, I leave that hell, and come here full of hopes. And this turns out to be another hell; the worship of money is as bad as the worst in Cuba. All these years, I've felt Manhattan was just another island-jail. A bigger jail with more distractions but a jail nonetheless. It just goes to show that there are more than two hells. I left one kind of hell behind and fell into another kind. I never thought I would live to see us plunge again into the dark ages. This plague—AIDS—is but a symptom of the sickness of our age."

As night fell, the neon of the billboards of midtown Manhattan and the lights of the skyscrapers provided the only illumination. We chatted in hushed tones, more intimately than we ever had before. I was aware of how precious the moment was to me, how I wanted to engrave it forever in my memory. When I got up to leave, Reinaldo had difficulty finding his slippers in the darkness, so I knelt on the floor and put them on his calloused, swollen, plum-colored feet. We went again through the kitchen, where he mentioned he would have broiled fish for dinner. Then he unchained the numerous locks, slowly, one by one. We didn't hug or shake hands as we parted—as if neither of those gestures was appropriate.

"Call me any time, if you need anything," I said.

"You're such a dear," he said.

As I was about to take the first step down, I turned around. The door to the apartment was still open. In the rectangular darkness Reinaldo's shadowy shape was like a ghost who couldn't make up its mind whether to materialize or to vanish.

The following day Reinaldo called to ask me if I could get him some grass. He said he had heard it helped to control nausea after meals. I told him that I would try to get some. I called a couple of friends and mentioned Reinaldo's request. Bill Sullivan suggested that I contact the Gay Men's Health Crisis because he thought Reinaldo sounded suicidal. I dismissed this possibility. Because his wish was to die by the sea, I thought he would try to make it to Puerto Rico if he received the grant from PEN. The next day, around noon, Tom Colchie called to say that Reinaldo had taken his life the night before; that he had used pills and had washed them down with shots of Chivas Regal; that he had left letters—one of them for the police, clarifying the circumstances of his death—and another one for the Cuban exiles, urging them to continue their fight against Castro's rule. Reinaldo had died in the early hours of December 7, and his body had been found by the woman who came by to help with his chores. He was forty-seven.

On December 19, at a Catholic church in Manhattan, a handful of Reinaldo's friends attended a mass in his honor. A couple of people eulogized him. His friend, the Barnard professor Perla Rozencvaig, talked about how even though Reinaldo did not attend church, he was very religious. The next orator was Lázaro Carriles, who recited one of Reinaldo's poems, celebrating death in the tradition of Góngora and St. John of the Cross. He finished with a poem also about the triumph of death, by Manuel Gutiérrez Nájera, a nineteenth-century Mexican poet, a poem that, he informed us, Reinaldo loved:

> I want to die as the day declines
> In the open sea and facing the sky
> Where agony will seem like a dream
> And the soul a bird taking flight.
>
> Not to listen in the last instants
> —Now alone with the sea and the sky—
> To other voices or tearful prayers
> Than the majestic tumble of the waves.
>
> To die when the sad light withdraws
> Its gilded nets from the green sea
> And to be like the sun that slowly sinks
> Something very luminous going under.
>
> To die, and young: before treacherous
> Time withers the graceful crown;
> When life still says I am all yours
> although we know it will betray us.

A man in a dark suit and carrying a briefcase sat in front of me; he seemed to be seething with anger and quite determined to hold back his tears. After Lázaro Carriles finished the poem, the priest tried as best as he could to rationalize Reinaldo's suicide, implying that perhaps Reinaldo was not aware of the enormity of this action for a believer. But all of us present knew perfectly well that in the last terrible act of his life Reinaldo Arenas had been fully aware of what he was doing.

4

Federico García Lorca
and Internalized Homophobia

I came to terms with my own internalized homophobia only after Manuel
and Reinaldo and other close friends died of AIDS. In a way, I can say that
it was because of AIDS that I finally learned to love gay men as soul mates.

I did not come out of the closet easily. After I was graduated from college, I moved to Colombia as much to become a writer as to get as far from
my family as possible; I believed they would disapprove of my homosexuality. Colombia seemed the logical place: a college professor of mine had
moved to Bogotá to direct an ecumenical agency, and he offered me a job
as a liaison between the Catholic church and the Protestant churches.

In Bogotá, where I had cousins I seldom saw, I hoped to hide my
homosexuality in a city of several million people. Hide it I did. Though
my employer and my new friends were liberals, nonhomophobic people, I
couldn't come out to them. I only felt comfortable doing so with other gay
men. But because of the fear I had of being "found out," I started feeling
like a criminal and began to use drugs heavily to escape an anxiety that
nothing quelled.

For the next fifteen years, high on drugs and alcohol on a daily basis,
I lived in a world where most of the important people in my life were
homosexuals. Although at one point I shared my life with another man
for sixteen years, and my family knew about us, it was still hard for me to
be openly gay in front of many friends from earlier periods of my life. In
those fifteen years, though I wrote a few explicit homosexual poems and
touched upon homosexuality in my fiction, I did not identify myself (except for occasional publications in little-known homosexual journals) as
a gay man. The images that appeared of homosexuality in my work were
very warped: like García Lorca, violence and homosexual self-hatred were
beneath everything I wrote. To me, being a gay man meant partying with

men and having sex with them—whatever love I felt for men was deeply submerged. At best, men could be friends. The great majority of them were nothing more than sex toys.

After Manuel and Reinaldo died, I was plunged into the bleakest depression of my life. The year I turned forty I emerged from a bacterial infection that nearly destroyed my lungs and brought me closer to death than I had ever been before.

A reevaluation of the life I had lived up until that moment took place. I started to recover from the devastation the years of heavy drinking and drug use had wreaked on my self-esteem and on my career as a writer. I became a college teacher and, after years of producing stillborn stories and novels, I began to write about my homosexuality and found a new, more honest vein from which came my novel *Latin Moon in Manhattan* and the pieces I wrote about Manuel and Reinaldo that are included in this book. My poetry too experienced a rebirth.

In retrospect it seems only logical that during those years I turned to revisiting the work and the life of Federico García Lorca. He, Puig, and Arenas constitute the great triumvirate of openly homosexual writers who have written in Spanish. How I became seriously involved with Lorca, though, I owe to a fortuitous encounter.

In 1988 a friend called to ask me whether I would be interested in having dinner with Edouard Roditi, a French writer who was known in certain underground homosexual circles for having spent a night of love with Lorca in 1928, when Federico stopped in Paris on his way to New York. It seemed like too good an opportunity to pass up. Although by that point I had read Ian Gibson's official biography, and Paul Binding's critical examination of Lorca as a gay writer, I had never heard of anyone who had had homosexual contact with him. Gibson himself, in the introduction to the biography, laments that a veil fell on that subject soon after Lorca's death, and no survivors were willing to speak about that subject, on or off the record.

Roditi was by then an old man, and from what he told me during that dinner I wrote the following poem:

My Night with Federico García Lorca
(As told by Edouard Roditi)

It happened in Paris.
Pepe asked me over to dinner
to meet a guy named Federico
who was on his way to New York.

71

I was nineteen years old.
Federico was eleven years older
and had just finished
a relationship in Spain
with a sculptor
who had been rotten to him.
Federico only had two lovers—
he hated promiscuous queens.

We were both Gemini.
Since astrology
was very important to him,
Federico took an interest in me.
We spoke in Spanish.
I had learned it
from my grandmother, a Sephardic
Jew, who had taught me
sixteenth-century expressions.
Federico was amused by all this.

We drank a lot
of wine that night.
In the morning, when I woke up,
his head lay across my nipples.
Hundreds of people
have asked me for details:
Was Federico fabulous in bed?
I always give them my standard answer:
Federico was emotional
and vulnerable; for him,
the most important thing wasn't sex
but tenderness.

I never saw him again.
The following day he left for England
then New York and Cuba.
Later, the second love
of his life was murdered
defending the Republic.

All this happened in Paris
almost sixty years ago.
It was just a night of love
but it has lasted all my life.

Shortly after I published this poem in a gay magazine, I was surprised to
hear from many people who loved it. I read it at a couple of readings later
that year, and, before I knew it, it had become a sort of signature piece and

made me an "authority" on Lorca. It was then that I went back to rereading and rethinking him, something I had not ever anticipated would happen.

I turned to the work of Lorca that I had read during my college years and that had given me a new appreciation of him as an artist and as a man: *Poet in New York,* specifically the poem that most openly dealt with Lorca's knowledge of homosexual life, *Ode to Walt Whitman.* During my college years I had discovered another Lorca, different from the poet I had ridiculed as an adolescent: the playwright of such powerful modern works as *Blood Wedding, Yerma,* and *The House of Bernarda Alba.* During those years I read Allen Ginsberg's *Howl,* which contains a poem—"A Supermarket in California"—addressed, at one point, to Walt Whitman, who is "eyeing" the grocery boys in a supermarket. Another part of the poem refers to García Lorca: "and you, / García Lorca, what are you doing down by the watermelons?"

The context in which these lines appear seemed to imply that Lorca had been homosexual. Shortly afterward, I reread Lorca's *Poet in New York,* and my perception of him was radically changed. Moreover, after reading *Ode to Walt Whitman,* I realized it was a poem that was knowledgeable about different homosexual communities in the Spanish-speaking world.

All the evidence indicates that Lorca completed the first known draft of his *Ode to Walt Whitman* (dated June 1930) after he left New York for Cuba. (The poem never appeared in Spain during Lorca's lifetime.) That poem, more than any other, speaks about Lorca's homosexual experience and of his experiences as a homosexual in New York City. The first time I read it, I was shocked by its in-your-face explicitness. Reading it as a forty-year-old man, it was hard for me not to read into it Lorca's internalized homophobia and self-hatred.

The poem is a remarkable document that explores, among other themes, Lorca's hatred of New York: "New York of slime / New York of wires and death." The other major theme of the poem is Lorca's love of Whitman's persona, his eroticization and idealization of the poet. In contrast to his hatred of Gotham, Lorca sings his love of Whitman. Repeatedly, Lorca calls him "beautiful Walt Whitman," and praises Whitman's "thighs of Virginal Apollo," and his voice "ancient and beautiful as the mist." Lorca goes on to call Whitman "Adam of blood, male, / lone man in the sea."

To this virile image of Whitman, Lorca contrasts New York's effete homosexuals, whom he calls pansies: "pouring out of sewers in bunches, / trembling between the legs of chauffeurs / or revolving on the platforms of absinthe." These pansies, "muddy with fears, flesh for whip," "of tumescent flesh and unclean mind" dare dream of Walt Whitman and defile Whitman's "chaste and luminous beard."

73

Lorca sympathizes, though, with gay men in the closet: "I do not raise my voice . . . against . . . the boy who dresses himself in the bride's trousseau / in the darkness of the wardrobe, / . . . nor the lonely men in clubs . . . nor the men with a green stare / who love and burn their lips in silence." What Lorca has trouble with is the fairies of all nations: *pájaros* of Havana, *jotos* of Mexico, *sarasas* of Cádiz, and so on. These homosexuals are the "murderers of doves! / Women's slaves, bitches of the boudoirs." To them, Lorca gives no quarter because "death / flows from your eyes."

Biographers and Lorquian scholars alike have tried to dilute with apologetic explanations the poem's distinctly homophobic language, but Lorca's attitude toward "pansies" can be understood if we take into account that New York City may have been both liberating and threatening to him. In his *Village Voice* article "The Way We Were: Gay Male Society in the Jazz Age," George Chauncey, Jr., writes, "The effeminate homosexual men, usually called 'fairies'—who managed to be flamboyant even in a suit— were the most visible element of gay male life. They not only dominated public stereotypes but set the tone within the gay world much more in the '20s than they do today." He adds, "More gay men in the 1920s than today *did* adopt effeminate mannerisms: they provided one of the few sure means of announcing one's sexuality. But acting like a 'fairy' was more than just a code; it was the dominant role model available to men forming a gay identity, and one against which almost every gay man had to measure himself. The culture of effeminacy provided remarkable support to men who rejected the kind of masculinity ascribed to them by the dominant society, but it also alienated many others for whom effeminate behavior would have been inauthentic and unacceptable."

Federico's friends and acquaintances all seem to agree that the Andalusian was manly, yet many photographs we have of him show a distinctly effeminate side. In the *Ode to Walt Whitman* Lorca might have been expressing a subconscious self-hatred. Ian Gibson quotes an account stating that Lorca was not an "obvious" homosexual. Also, the Guatemalan poet Luis Cardoza y Aragón, who knew Federico in Cuba, wrote that the Andalusian poet was not even slightly effeminate. Considering that in the Spanish-speaking world there was only one known type of homosexual— the fairy-queen-pansy-effeminate type—Lorca may have deliberately cultivated a manly manner, which on occasion he let down. Yet in *Ode to Walt Whitman* Lorca addresses Walt Whitman as one homosexual talking to another. It's possible that by spewing out his hatred for urban effeminate gays Lorca may have opened room in his psyche to begin to come to terms with his own homosexuality.

What exactly were the circumstances that had brought Federico to this point in his evolution as a gay man where he rejected all but the masculine types? To find the answer one would have to go back to Federico's move from Granada to Madrid in his midtwenties to study at the Residencia de Estudiantes.

The Residencia was an upper-level educational institution based on the English tutorial system of Oxford and Cambridge. With patrons such as King Alfonso XIII, and the most notable Spanish intellectuals of the time, the Residencia attracted many of Spain's brightest young minds. Here Federico met the surrealist filmmaker Luis Buñuel. This is how Buñuel describes the Lorca of those years, in *My Last Sigh,* Buñuel's autobiography: "Federico was brilliant and charming, with a visible desire for sartorial elegance—his ties were always in impeccable taste. With his dark, shining eyes, he had a magnetism that few could resist. . . . (Perhaps our mutual attraction was at least in part due to our differences.) . . . I remember someone once telling me that a man . . . was spreading the rumor that Lorca was a homosexual, a charge I found impossible to believe."

"There was absolutely nothing effeminate or affected about Federico," Buñuel adds, noting that Federico "despised" any kind of flamboyant display of homosexuality (which is ironic because Lorca looks exceedingly nelly in many photographs). Buñuel also noted that Lorca "had no tolerance for off-color jokes" about homosexuals. When Buñuel finally confronted Lorca about whether he was a *maricón,* Lorca's reply was "You and I are finished!" They weren't; their friendship lasted a few more years.

Lorca returned to his parents' home in Granada to receive his law degree in 1923. Then Federico persuaded his parents to allow him to return to the Residencia, where he met Salvador Dalí, who was his first great, and unrequited, love.

Dalí was eighteen when he arrived at the Residencia de Estudiantes. He was already a flamboyant dresser, a dandy, and painted in the cubist style. For a while Dalí, Buñuel, and Lorca became inseparable—the bond of genius uniting them. Lorca was six years older than the painter. Luis Buñuel tells us that "Lorca nurtured quite a grand passion for Dalí [who] . . . remained unmoved." This initial crush would blossom in the next few years. For his part, Dalí was equally—but not erotically—impressed by Federico (or so Dalí would want us to believe). Dalí, who never acknowledged being a homosexual, cultivated an androgynous persona. However, in the public's mind he was linked to Gala, his wife. In later life Dalí surrounded himself with homosexuals, especially drag queens with whom he had affairs. (Crysis International, the transsexual actress-singer who died in 1988, claimed that she and Dalí were lovers.)

As astonishing as Dalí's appearance was—huge hats, velvet capes, canes, and an outlandish moustache were among his props—Lorca himself was already in those years a formidable character. About the young Federico, Luis Buñuel wrote: "Of all the human beings I've ever known, Federico was the finest. I don't mean his plays or his poetry; I mean him personally. He was his own masterpiece. Whether sitting at the piano imitating Chopin, improvising a pantomime, or acting out a scene from a play, he was irresistible. He read beautifully, and he had passion, youth and joy. . . . He was like a flame."

Eventually, Lorca returned to Granada and Dalí to his hometown, Figueras, in Catalonia. If they corresponded, none of the letters is extant. A year went by before they saw each other again. Easter 1925, Federico received an invitation to visit Salvador Dalí at his family's homes in Figueras (the Dalí family's main residence) and in Cadaqués, where they summered. Cadaqués is a picturesque village on the Mediterranean, a few miles from the French border on Spain's Costa Brava. There, it is said, in the tiny bay of Port Lligat, Dalí would sometimes come to the beach in the late afternoons—naked beneath a sheet—for erotic encounters with local fishermen.

Federico's visit to Dalí in 1925 seems to have been an idyllic time for the two young men. Dalí made sketches of the poet, which he later used to paint the canvases *Invitation to Dream* (1926), and *Honey Is Sweeter Than Blood,* both now lost. In turn, Federico—a gifted watercolorist and draftsman—sketched the painter. There is a photograph of the pair wearing bathing suits at the beach, Federico sitting, Dalí standing behind him. Federico's left hand rests on one of Dalí's knees. This is, unmistakably, a photograph of two men deeply involved with each other.

Shortly after he left Cadaqués, Lorca began writing the "Ode to Salvador Dalí," a poem of twenty-eight stanzas. In its final seven stanzas Lorca manages to articulate (albeit cryptically) the true nature of his feelings for Dalí. The line "Oh Salvador Dalí, of the olive-colored voice!" in the twenty-second stanza is the first verse that has a distinctly sensual connotation, but the qualities Lorca goes on to name next—"halting adolescent brush . . . longing for eternity"—seem to be more artistic or metaphysical attributes than sexual ones. It isn't until the twenty-fifth stanza that Lorca finally musters the courage to say:

> But above all I sing a common thought
> that joins us in the dark and golden hours.
> The light that blinds our eyes is not art.
> Rather it is love, friendship, crossed swords.

Maybe it was to sublimate their relationship that Dalí did a painting of himself being penetrated by Lorca.

The American biographer Jeffrey Hogrefe, who is at work on a biography of Dalí, told me that the painter had a lengthy homosexual relationship with Edward James, an Englishman who was a patron of the arts. Hogrefe also met a young man in Cadaqués who declared he had had sexual encounters with the painter. Furthermore, there are many accounts of straight men who say Dalí tried to seduce them.

Hogrefe claims that, like Andy Warhol, Dalí was squeamish about sexual matters — he disliked being touched by anyone. Although Dalí did have a deep bond with Gala, he acknowledged having sex with her only once, when they first met. He did, however, encourage her to have sex with other men. Dalí acknowledged he was a masochist and that Gala was his dominatrix. Even though many gay men fell in love with Dalí, he was only interested in heterosexual men who were rough types. Dalí was also a voyeur. He enjoyed watching straight men make love to prostitutes and loved to stage heterosexual and homosexual orgies, in which he sometimes participated by masturbating.

Since "posing" was at the center of Dalí's being, it's understandable that he may have wanted the public to have an ambiguous image of his sexuality. Dalí did not requite Lorca's love.

Federico became depressed. Around this time the twenty-seven-year-old Lorca, began to talk about his desire to leave Spain and travel in Europe. Federico may have thought that in the great metropolises — London, Berlin, Paris, Rome — which had large homosexual populations, he could find comradeship, sexual happiness.

For the next two years Federico lived between Granada and Madrid, returning to Madrid for a short stay at the Residencia. This is the period of his greatest intimacy with Dalí, and they saw each other often. That same summer the two men saw each other in Cadaqués, and Lorca held an exhibition of his drawings in Barcelona. The drawings were not well received, either by the critics or the public. Lorca's lovely homoerotic drawings are obsessed with depicting wounded pierrots and sailors.

In the autumn of 1927 Lorca's *Mariana Pineda* opened in Madrid to favorable reviews. What also made 1927 a watershed year in Federico's life was his deepening involvement with the sculptor Emilio Aladrén Perojo. One of the poems in *Gypsy Ballads,* "Ballad of the Marked Man," is dedicated to Aladrén Perojo. The poem is written in a slightly different mode from the rest of the poems in the volume, its images more surrealistic and faintly homoerotic: "Dense oxen of water / charge at the boys / bathing in the moons / of their rippling horns." The ballad, about a man named Amargo, doesn't seem to comment in any way on Lorca's relationship with Aladrén. The two men had met three years earlier, and about this time Lorca, finally realizing that Dalí was never going to reciprocate his passion, became closer to Aladrén Perojo. Lorca was eight years older than Aladrén Perojo, a dark beauty whose refined features were similar to Dalí's.

Federico paraded the sculptor around the artistic circles of Madrid and Granada where Lorca's many male admirers were jealous of Aladrén Perojo, who apparently had a terrible temper and was not averse to creating public rows. Two of Lorca's friends from that period have spoken briefly of the relationship. José María García Carrillo once confided to the diarist Agustín Peñón that Aladrén Perojo "was Federico's great love." The writer Rafael Martínez Nadal is quoted in Ian Gibson's biography as saying that "Lorca took Aladrén everywhere, introduced him to everybody and found him, for several years, a source of joy." Aladrén Perojo died in 1944, leaving a few letters to Lorca, though none from the poet to Aladrén is extant.

Gypsy Ballads, Lorca's volume of poems, went through several printings soon after publication, an unknown phenomenon in Spain. The reviews were glowing. However, Salvador Dalí had reservations about *Gypsy Ballads.* Although Dalí said he admired the book, he wrote a letter to Lorca encouraging him to give up folklore rhyme. Dalí predicted the result would be an unequaled poetic intensity. (When Lorca followed Dalí's advice two years later, in *Poet in New York,* he wrote his first modern work.) Buñuel commented that he had found splendid images in Lorca's book, but he was appalled by its narrative nature.

Despite his success, Lorca was unhappy. To the Colombian poet Jorge Zalamea he wrote complaining about his low spirits. Federico must have felt a failure in love. Emilio Aladrén was apparently bisexual (or afraid of fully assuming his homosexuality in Spanish society). Around that time Aladrén started to become involved with the woman who would become his wife.

Meantime, Dalí had moved to Paris, and he began to collaborate with Buñuel. The famous and influential surrealist film they made, *Un Chien Andalou* (Andalusian dog), deeply upset Lorca. Back then Andalusians often were referred to as *los perros andaluces* (Andalusian dogs). Lorca thought the title was an insulting allusion to him. I saw the film again recently. I tried as hard as I could, but I could not detect any slights, or even references, to Federico.

Because Lorca was depressed, his parents gave him their permission in 1929 for his first trip to the Americas. Federico was thirty-one and still financially dependent on his parents. He chose New York where his old professor and friend Fernando de los Ríos was scheduled to give a series of lectures at Columbia University.

Like many avant-garde young intellectuals of his generation, Federico was fascinated by black culture and the movies. He was particularly captivated with the American comedian Buster Keaton and wrote a short screenplay titled "Buster Keaton's Outing." The United States—where the cinema and jazz were born—represented the future. Like Dalí and Buñuel, Federico could have gone to Paris, but he might have stayed away from Paris because his two estranged friends had developed an intimacy that excluded him. The painter and the filmmaker had already begun to make names for themselves on the international artistic scene, whereas Federico was still unknown outside Spain, except for small circles of Hispanic poets in New York and Latin America.

Federico wrote to the Chilean diplomat Carlos Mora Lynch, saying he was going to New York because it was the worst of all the places he could think of visiting. Of all the reasons he could have given, that is among the least convincing. Obviously, one lure of New York was that it is in the Americas; another was that from New York Federico could travel to Cuba, which he had dreamed of visiting since his childhood. Also, he might have chosen New York because then, as now, New York was known as a mecca for homosexuals; they flock to Gotham to escape the narrow-mindedness of their small hometowns or, in Lorca's case, the narrow-mindedness of an entire culture.

Before traveling to New York, Lorca read Walt Whitman's poetry in translation. An anthology of Whitman's poetry had appeared in Spain in 1912, and the young poets in Madrid adopted Whitman. Whitman's poems of homosexual love in *Calamus* had made a profound impression on Lorca, as witnessed by the *Ode to Walt Whitman*. No other poet (Cavafy's poetry was still unknown in Spain) had written more explicitly about his love for men. In "I Sing the Body Electric," Whitman had proclaimed, "To see him pass conveys as much as the best poem, perhaps more." In "For You O Democracy," Whitman had stated, "I will make divine magnetic lands / With the love of comrades, / With the life-long love of comrades." In "I Hear It Was Charged Against Me," Whitman wrote, "Only I will establish in the Mannahatta and in every city of these States island and seaboard, / And in the fields and woods, and above every keel little or large that dents the water, / Without edifices or rules or trustees or any argument, / The institution of the dear love of comrades." And, most boldly, in a visionary vein Whitman had written in "I Dream'd in a Dream":

I dream'd in a dream I saw a city invincible to the
    attacks of the
whole of the rest of the earth,
I dream'd that was the new city of Friends,
Nothing was greater there than the quality of robust
    love, it led the rest,
It was seen every hour in the actions of the men of
    that city,
And in all their looks and words.

For Lorca, whose passion for men was mostly unrequited, these poems may have awakened a strong desire to travel to a land where the love of men seemed a possibility.

On June 12, 1929, Federico, accompanied by Fernando de los Ríos, boarded the train to Paris. Philip Cummings, a twenty-one-year-old American student whom Federico had met at the Residencia, was on the same train. Here is Philip Cummings's description of meeting Lorca for the first time at the Residencia: "One warm afternoon in Madrid I sat on the bench overlooking the city from the Residencia when I was aroused by singing and a music which seemed pregnant with the orange sunshine of Andalusia and to bear the great and melancholy motives of the strange plateaus to the north of Medina del Campo. Looking into the *Sala de Conferencias* I saw a young, olive-skinned man playing without music, and singing words which moved his distinguished audience of professors."

Federico and his party stayed only one night in Paris before sailing for England. (That was the night that the writer Edouard Roditi met him and slept with him.) The following day Lorca and his party, minus Philip Cummings, went to England, and after a short stay of a few days they sailed for New York, arriving June 25.

The Roaring Twenties were coming to an end, and Lorca could not have chosen a more interesting time to arrive in the United States. Prohibition was still in effect; the stock market crash of 1929 was imminent. It was also the age of jazz, the Harlem renaissance, the first talkies, and infamous gangsters.

Lorca, who was by then a famous poet in Hispanic circles, had admirers impatiently awaiting his arrival. When his ship, the *Olympic,* docked in Manhattan, intellectuals, poets, journalists, and other admirers were there to meet him.

Lorca enrolled at Columbia University to study English and took up residence at Furnald Hall.

New York City already had an exciting gay culture. Gays had their own meetingplaces, neighborhoods, and even dress codes. Federico lost no time finding his way to Harlem where the Rockland Palace, Harlem's biggest dance hall, hosted huge and lavish drag balls. In the poem "The King of Harlem," one wonders whether the lines "Ah, masqueraded Harlem! / Ah, Harlem, threatened by a mob wearing clothes without heads!" refer to the drag balls that Lorca may have attended. Greenwich Village was already a gay neighborhood, and the speakeasies of Times Square were notorious hangouts for gays. Not far from Columbia University was the Soldiers' and Sailors' Monument at Riverside Drive and 79th Street, a place that had a reputation for lively cruising. However, cruising was dangerous. In 1926, as George Chauncey informs us in his *Village Voice* article, "More than 600 men were arrested for cruising in the city's parks, subway washrooms, and public squares." Even so, New York's gay life had to be a more stimulating atmosphere for Lorca than the repressed gay world of Spain.

No one knows what plays Federico saw in New York. But at that time the American theater was beginning to address homosexual themes and to stage explicit plays, which sometimes were raided by the police.

Federico contacted Philip Cummings and on August 19 took a train to Montepelier, Vermont, to visit him. Federico was delighted to get away from the sweltering pavement of Manhattan in August.

There was nothing to suggest that Lorca and Philip Cummings were anything but friends. It was always reported that the two young men were good friends, confidants. Lorca gave Cummings a packet with private papers that he asked him to keep in a safe place. In 1961 Cummings opened that packet and found a note from Federico begging Cummings to destroy the packet if he hadn't heard from the poet in ten years. Cummings complied.

Whether Lorca and Cummings had a sexual relationship was an open question. Even if their relationship was platonic, one could perhaps safely assume that the two young men had crushes on one another. Nevertheless, an erotic connection between them is clear in pictures of them together. These photographs provide important material for decoding. When Lorca poses with a woman, or with a group of people, the dynamics are different than when he poses alone, or with some of the important men in his life. In one photograph, taken in Vermont, the two young men are standing next to each other. Federico holds a basket of flowers, and his shoulder is pressing under Cummings's armpit; Cummings had draped his arm around Federico's shoulder. Federico looks like a beautiful *señorita*. It's impossible to look at that photo and not notice how delicate, how feminine, Lorca could be at times.

That picture was all the evidence I needed of their intimate relationship. But I couldn't offer my interpretation as fact. Then, in the winter of

1997, I ran into the Spanish poet and academic Dionisio Cañas whom I hadn't seen in more than a decade. He had read my book of poems, *My Night with Federico García Lorca*. Cañas said, "I *almost* had a night with Federico: I went to bed with Philip Cummings!" This was the first time I had heard about Cummings's homosexuality. According to Cañas, in 1986 he was in Vermont with friends, near Lake Eden where Lorca had visited the cottage of the Cummings family. On a whim Cañas called information to see if anybody named Philip Cummings was living in the area. A man by the name of Philip Cummings was listed in Woodstock, near Eden Mills. Cañas and his friends went by the house to pay him a visit. It was the same man who had known Lorca. Philip Cummings was seventy-five and white haired, no longer the slim young blond that we know from the pictures of 1922, but he still spoke excellent Spanish. A widower living alone, he received the unexpected visitors graciously and regaled them with anecdotes. As Cañas and his friends were preparing to leave, Cummings called Cañas (then thirty-six) aside and told him he would like to see him again, alone.

Cummings and Cañas corresponded for a few months. In one letter Cummings derides both the academics interested in Lorca and Lorca's family for never wanting to acknowledge the true nature of the relationship between the two men.

The night Dionisio Cañas arrived for their private visit, Cummings spoke frankly about the nature of his relationship with Lorca. The two had been not friends, he said, but *novios* (boyfriends). They had started a sexual relationship in Spain, and it continued in America. Cummings claimed he visited Lorca once in Granada. Philip Cummings had never mentioned any of this to the Lorca biographers or scholars who had interviewed him because by then he was a closeted married man with children and because Lorca's biographers have been mainly heterosexuals not interested in exploring in depth the nature of Lorca's sexuality. But now that his wife was dead, his children grown, and Cummings himself an old man, he was ready to talk to Cañas *"de todo"* (about everything).

That night, dressed in a kimono, he seduced Cañas, who says he went to bed with Cummings because it was the closest he could come to being with Lorca. Cummings revealed many intimate details about Federico. Dionisio Cañas has written that "on one occasion Lorca told Philip that he was afraid of his brother Francisco, of his catholicism, and that he [the brother] made sure that Federico always looked good in society. Meaning that he did not flaunt his homosexuality." In addition to saying that Lorca had *"una polla muy grande"* (a very big dick), and was *"muy buena"* (very good), Cummings told Cañas that Lorca was *"un español caliente"* (a passionate Spaniard). Lorca, according to Cummings, had been despondent during his visit to Lake Eden and wrote a memoir condemning Dalí and Buñuel, who ridiculed Lorca's homosexuality and mocked his aesthetics.

Now that we know the true nature of their relationship, it is finally possible to read "Double Poem of Lake Eden" as a text in which Lorca wrestles bitterly with his homosexual passion and with the man he has become: "My old voice / was ignorant of the thick and bitter sap. . . . Oh, ancient voice of my love, / oh, voice of my truth." These verses seem to imply that the poet feels disillusioned with love—that his old voice, the voice of his youth, was that of a homosexual who had not yet experienced the pain of rejection. It's possible that the American is the love to whom the poem alludes, a love that is lost now that Cummings is back in Vermont and back in the closet. The poem displays a tension between the man Lorca really is and the man he has to be in the eyes of society. Walking in the woods surrounding Lake Eden, Lorca feels his pagan spirits revive, and he curses "Little men with horns" who do not allow him to live in "the grove of leisure / and the somersaults of pure joy." Here Federico seems to be condemning Christianity, which sees the nature of all sin as emanating from Adam and Eve's making love in the garden of Eden.

Lorca had become tired of subterfuges. In the sixth stanza of the poem he cries out, "I want my liberty, my human love." He implores his old, innocent self to "burn with your tongue . . . this voice of tin."

"Double Poem of Lake Eden" also contains some of the most beautiful and heartfelt verses Lorca wrote: "I am not a man, nor a poet, nor a leaf, / but a wounded pulse that circles the unknown," he says of his desire to explore a subject like sexuality, which was taboo in Spanish American literature before he came along. Toward the end of the poem Lorca insists all he wants is to cry like "a passionate man / who kills mockery and concealment." Then he howls, "I desire . . . my body floats pulled by the opposites."

Federico stayed at Columbia University until the following January. In October the stock market crashed, precipitating the Great Depression. That same month Lorca wrote to his parents that he was at work on an avant-garde play. It seems likely that it was around this time that he conceived of the idea for *The Public,* the most daring and openly homosexual play he ever wrote.

In New York City Federico had begun to feel liberated enough to start addressing homosexuality in his writing. In this sense, New York was of monumental importance in his development. But despite the friends he made, parties he attended, great events he witnessed, attention he received, great jazz he listened to, and thrilling plays and movies he saw, it's safe to say that Lorca was often despondent in New York. The poem "Christmas," which he wrote in February 1930, speaks to that effect: "I have spent the whole night among the scaffolds of the outskirts . . . / What matters is this: Emptiness. Solitary world. / Estuary."

Federico had crossed the Atlantic to forget his disappointment with his failed relationships with men, but it's likely that Federico continued to love Emilio Aladrén Perojo, that Dalí's betrayal still stung, and that Cummings, back in the closet, had disappointed him. From this anger and despair Lorca wrote the poems of *Poet in New York* and, most specifically, *Ode to Walt Whitman,* a work in which he spewed the homophobic self-hatred he felt at having been betrayed by the homosexual men he had loved and in which he vented his feeling about being an outcast in the stereotyped world of gay New York.

From New York Federico went to Cuba, where he was charmed by the black men of the island. In his biography of Lorca, Ian Gibson writes, "As for the mulatto youths, with their chocolate-colored skin and breathtaking bodies, Lorca was by all accounts almost speechless with admiration; and . . . he soon began to pursue them."

Lorca, who wrote his *Ode to Walt Whitman* and his one homosexual play, *The Public,* in Cuba, finally came out of the closet in Havana. Perhaps the experience of New York's vast homosexual demimonde helped him to become public about his sexuality. Luis Cardoza y Aragón has written that one day he visited Lorca at the hotel where he was staying in Havana and found Federico in bed, surrounded by a cluster of adoring fans.

In Havana Lorca met the homosexual Colombian poet Porfirio Barba Jacob, the most important homosexual poet in Latin American literature. Born in 1883, Barba Jacob led a wandering life, changing his name three times (his real name was Miguel Angel Osorio) and suffering incarceration, bankruptcy, exile, and ostracism. In his role as Latin America's revolutionary and doomed poet, Barba Jacob wrote openly about his homosexuality, drug addiction, and alcoholism. A criminal genius on the order of Jean Genet, Barba Jacob was, unlike Lorca, public about his sexual preferences. In his life, and in his poetry, the Colombian was unafraid of expressing his love for men and willing to suffer the consequences of being out of the closet. Certainly, tender and lyrical verses such as "Give me your honey, child of the perfumed mouth!" may have been an influence on the passionate *Sonnets of Dark Love* that Lorca wrote toward the end of his life.

When he wasn't socializing, Lorca worked on *The Public*—his most outrageous and boldest work. He must have had great confidence in himself at this point because he read parts of this play to the Loynaza family, an artistic family that befriended him and opened their home to him.

The visit to New York had helped Lorca to find his voice; his reputation as an important and original author rests on the works he wrote subsequently. In Gotham Federico began to think about the poems that later became part of *Poet in New York,* and that liberating impulse reached its most powerful manifestation in the surrealist plays *The Public* and *Once Five Years Pass.* Neither play was ever performed in the poet's lifetime, although Federico read from *The Public* to some of his closest friends in Madrid shortly before his death. It's easy to see why this play had to wait for publication until 1976: it is a ferocious homosexual work that Franco's censorship would have persecuted as immoral.

In his autobiography, *My Last Sigh,* Luis Buñuel wrote: "The real purpose of surrealism was not to create a new literary, artistic or even philosophical movement, but to explode the social order, to transform life itself." Perhaps the most daring and revolutionary of all of Lorca's works, *The Public,* seems, even today, both in terms of its style and its content, a play of dazzling audacity. A non-narrative surrealist/absurdist work, it is difficult to stage and even to describe. Lorca called it "a poem for booing." It deals with a production of *Romeo and Juliet,* in which Romeo is a man of thirty and Juliet is a boy of sixteen. The bourgeois public becomes incensed by the liberties taken with the classical theme, and the revolutionary students have to defend the production. The performance is disrupted by a riot.

The play addresses the meaning of love in life and in the theater. Mirroring Lorca's bitterness about his two failed relationships, Juliet early in the play says, "It's a trick, love's word, a broken mirror, footsteps in the water." Later, a student in the play comments, "And wherever love is talked about we'd run in there with our soccer shoes on, flinging mud all over the mirrors." But the Director, who could stand for Lorca's alter ego, also says, "I knew a man who'd sweep the roof and clean the skylights and railings only out of gallantry towards the sky." Later, to justify his iconoclastic production of *Romeo and Juliet,* the Director says, "For that reason I dared to perform an extremely difficult poetic trick in hopes that love would impetuously rip the costumes to shreds and then give them a new form."

Some of the major homosexual themes explored in *The Public* are crossdressing, transformation (whenever a male character is pushed behind the screen, he comes back out as a woman), and entrapment behind masks that will not allow homosexuals to be who they are, the masks that many Latino homosexuals have been forced to wear in private and in public. Of the crippling, life-denying effect of mask wearing, the Director states, "In the middle of the street, the mask buttons up and lets us avoid that indiscreet blush which sometimes rises to our cheeks. In the bedroom, when we stick our fingers in our nose or delicately explore our rear, the plaster of the mask presses down so heavily on our flesh that we're barely able to lie down in bed." Lorca is writing about how the public perception of gay people affects our private selves.

Through the leitmotif of the masks Lorca addresses the homosexual closet. The play can be read as an indictment of the men Lorca loved, men who chose to remain closeted rather than to express openly their true nature.

Homophobia is also portrayed in *The Public*. The character of the Centurion (who accompanies the Emperor in his search for homosexuals) says, upon finding two of them: "The emperor will guess which one of the two of you is one. With a knife or a gob of spit. May all of your kind be damned! It's your fault I'm roaming the roads and sleeping on the sand. My wife is beautiful, like a mountain. She gives birth out of four or five places at a time. . . . I've got two hundred children. And I'll still have many more. May your kind be damned!"

The play also touches on the themes of domination and bondage. The Character in Bells says to his lover, the Character in Vine Leaves: "Carry me to the bathtub and drown me. That's the only way you'll ever be able to see me naked. Do you imagine I'm afraid of blood? I know how to dominate you. Do you think I don't know you? To dominate you so completely that if I were to say, 'If I turned into a moon-fish?' you'd answer, 'I'd turn into a sack of little fish eggs.' "

And a little later on:

CHARACTER IN VINE LEAVES: Don't whip me!
CHARACTER IN BELLS: A whip made of ship's cables.
CHARACTER IN VINE LEAVES: Don't whip me on the belly!

When the Emperor enters in the next scene, the Character in Vine Leaves says to him: "If you kiss me I'll open my mouth so you can drive your sword into my neck afterwards."

The Public is Lorca's most fearless grappling with homosexuality in dramatic terms, but violence and homosexuality still seem to be synonymous in the Spaniard's mind. Lorca had yet to begin to fathom that tenderness and compassion can be found in the love of men. The only legitimate mode of discourse equated homosexuality with torment, pain, destruction, and sadomasochistic violence.

In Cuba Federico had come out of the closet both as a man and as an artist. Manuel Puig once said that many Latin American writers lived abroad so that they would not have to self-censor their work. It seems that Federico had to leave Spain in order to free himself from its morality.

One of his New York friends, Norma Brickell, wrote to her friend Mildred Adams after meeting Lorca aboard the ship that docked in New York harbor on its way back to Spain from Cuba that Federico had changed, that it was better Mildred did not see the coarse male he had become.

Perhaps she was more comfortable with a closeted Federico. When he stopped being discreet, he may have become threatening—even socially unacceptable—to many people.

In the next six years Federico would complete *Once Five Years Pass* and his three most famous plays, *Yerma, Blood Wedding,* and *The House of Bernarda Alba,* as well as the *Sonnets of Dark Love* (arguably his greatest love poetry).

The Spain to which Federico returned had also undergone a transformation. Soon the country would enter a civil war in which half a million people would die; Federico himself would be one of its victims.

After spending the summer with his family, Federico moved back to Madrid in October, where he resumed his relationship with Emilio Aladrén; everything seems to indicate that the passion between them had cooled. Federico gave readings of *The Public* to his friends and acquaintances, but the consensus was that the play was too incendiary to be staged in Spain.

During the summer of 1931, in Granada, Lorca worked on the experimental and symbolic play *Once Five Years Pass* and began to work on the first draft of *Blood Wedding.* Finally writing without having to censor himself, Lorca's creativity was flowing like a fountain. Writing morning, noon, and night, he was in the midst of his greatest achievement as a writer.

In August, at his parents' farm outside Granada, La Huerta de San Vicente, Lorca finished writing *Once Five Years Pass,* which he had started in New York. This work is both a safer and a more radical play than *The Public.* Whereas *The Public* contains shocking speeches and actions and aims to shake the smugness of middle-class theater goers, *Once Five Years Pass* has a dreamy, lyrical surface, and the tragic feelings it depicts are expressed with heartbreaking tenderness. Because both plays dare to dream of utopias unknown, their visionary nature puts them ahead of their time and of ours. Playfully fluid, *Once Five Years Pass* could be staged as a satirical and amusing comedy of manners, though its theme (the sterility of a life in the closet) made it unperformable when Lorca wrote it. Today this theme seems old-fashioned and quaint, but the play can be enjoyed for the lush splendor of the images Lorca has created for the stage and the moments when the characters express deep poetic feelings about the nature of desire.

Once Five Years Pass is the story of a young gay man engaged to marry a woman he doesn't love. Christopher Maurer has called it "the dramatization of a psychological journey." At the onset of the action the Old Man is talking to the Young Man, who seems to stand for Lorca's alter ego. The Young Man fans himself, indicating that he is not the typical Spanish macho. The pair is discussing the Young Man's fiancée, who has gone on a five-year trip with her family. The Young Man, who is "practically happy" that his bride has gone away, says, "For now, it's just not possible . . . for reasons I can't explain. I won't marry her . . . until five years pass!" The Old Man, who represents experience, and who has a more complete understanding of people, is glad that the Young Man has decided to wait, instead of getting married before he fully realizes that he's homosexual. The situation is still common in Latin culture: young men (especially those from the bourgeoisie) face a great deal of pressure to get married as soon as they reach maturity. The Young Man of Lorca's play is willing to comply with tradition, although he barely knows his fiancée. The Old Man has to correct him about her appearance: "Permit me to remind you that your fiancée . . . hasn't got braids." Undeterred, the Young Man calls his intended "my little girl, my child." The Old Man entreats him, "Try saying, my fiancée. Dare to!" But the Young Man is not able to do it, because he can see his betrothed only as a nonthreatening child, not as a full-grown woman with sexual desires. The Young Man wants, above all else, to live, which in his case means to accept his homosexual nature. That's why the Old Man advises him not to get married, because "the alternative is to die *right now*" (emphasis added).

The next character to enter is the Typist, a stereotype of a conventional woman of limited intelligence. She's in love with the Young Man. Talking about him, she confides to the Old Man, "When I was little, I used to watch him playing from my balcony. One day he fell, and his knee bled, you remember? That bright blood still trembles like a red snake between my breasts." However, she intuits the truth about him. She's not so much in love with him as with the convention of unrequited love. The Young Man reminds her that he "belongs to another," meaning that he belongs to his homosexuality. He further acknowledges that he would like to love her, if only he could. But the Old Man says, "By no means. Then what would you do tomorrow? Eh? think about it. Tomorrow!"

Everyone is suspicious of the Young Man. When a friend comes to visit, he asks, "And where are the pictures in this house of the girls you sleep with?" The Friend offers to introduce him to young women he knows, but the Young Man flatly refuses. Sensing the Young Man's confusion, the Friend teases him: "Yes, man, don't look so disgusted. A woman can be very ugly and a horse trainer beautiful, and vice versa, and . . . who knows?"

When the Young Man's fiancée appears in the second act, we are presented with Lorca's perhaps most independent and liberated female character. Indeed, she is one of the most powerfully sexual women in all Spanish literature—there's nothing repressed about her libido, and her mind is just as free as her sexual desires. The Fiancée is also a middle-class character who, like the Young Man, is expected to enter into a marriage of convenience to perpetuate the bourgeois tradition of having and raising a family. However, the Fiancée sees that her intended is really homosexual, and she doesn't want to marry a man who fans himself. She's ardently enamored of an American football player.

The kind of man the Fiancée wants represented an erotic ideal for Lorca. Soon after arriving in New York, Federico saw Columbia's football team play and became enamored of the sport. He wrote to his family describing the masculinity and beauty of the game, the sheer power of the players, and how it was not a game for frail people.

When the Football Player sneaks into the Fiancée's bedroom through her balcony, she kisses him and says, "White hot embers, ivory fire runs from your teeth! My other fiancée's teeth were cold; he'd kiss me and little withered leaves would cover his lips; what dry lips they were. I cut my braids because they pleased him, the same as I go barefoot because you like me that way. Isn't that true? Isn't it?"

Lorca implies that the Fiancée is no longer a virgin. When the Maid interrupts her with "Oh, miss!" the Fiancée replies, "What miss?" This dialogue is repeated again a little later in the scene in which the Maid (who is caught up in foolish romantic notions) defends the Young Man, calling him handsome. To which the Fiancée retorts: "Marry him yourself." The Fiancée can see through the Young Man's façade, and she refuses to play along with the conventions of society. When the Fiancée and the Maid discuss what she should wear to receive her intended, she refuses to wear a colorful dress; she doesn't want to look pretty for the Young Man. She says, "I want an earth-colored habit for that man, a habit of bare rock with a belt of hemp around the waist." What she is describing she wants to wear is the habit of a Franciscan monk. Later, when the Fiancée's father enters and asks her whether she's ready to meet her future husband, she replies, "I don't want to see him. I need to live." In other words, she refuses to live a lie, which is what Spanish society then demanded of gays and lesbians, and of heterosexual women, who in many instances were forced by their families to enter arranged marriages.

When the Young Man arrives, the Fiancée notices his "cold hand" and "old, old eyes." Immediately, he tries to turn the young woman into an icon and their relationship into conventional poetry: "It must have been the moonlight. It must have been the wind pressed into mouths to kiss your head." To these insincere advances she replies: "I don't want to dream. Nobody dreams here." Refusing to be his doll, she advises him to "find another woman to make braids for." When he realizes that she sees through him, the Young Man finally concedes, "It isn't your deceit that hurts. You are nothing. You mean nothing. It's my lost treasure, my purposeless love."

The Fiancée elopes with the Football Player. Searching for her, the Young Man runs into the Typist, who is willing to believe the clichés of his love rhetoric—she'd be content with an illusion if that's all she can have. She says to him, "Yes; I love you, but much more than that! You haven't got the eyes to see me naked, or the lips to kiss my never-ending body. Let me alone. I love you too much to even look at you!" She is saying that she loves him better in her imagination, that she would be happy never to consummate their "love." She is willing to be to him what the Fiancée refuses to be. They swear undying love to each other. At this point the Old Man, who represents truth, reappears. He wants to lead the Young Man away from this lie. Using symbolism to express his themes, Lorca ends the play with the shooting of the Young Man by a card player. As the Young Man dies, the Third Card Player screams, "One must never wait! One must live!"

Five Years was not performed in Lorca's lifetime, it is seldom staged, and it has never become part of the Lorca canon. Its main theme is the repression of one's sexual instincts (which is at the core of all Lorca's theater). Lorca seems to be admonishing the gay young men of his generation who preferred to go along with the conventions of 1930s Spain and who chose to conform and thus to die. Lorca himself refused to conform, but his process of liberation was long, arduous, and painful.

In 1931 the Republican government created the Misiones Pedagógicas, an organization designed to bring cultural activities to Spain's rural areas. Some students of the Residencia de Estudiantes came up with the idea of creating a traveling theater to bring Spanish peasants the works of Calderón de la Barca, Cervantes, Lope de Vega, and other classical authors. The students asked Lorca to become artistic director of the company. An overjoyed Lorca accepted.

The project became known as La Barraca (the barn). Subsidized by the Ministry of Education, La Barraca became a reality.

For the company's first tour Lorca chose to stage some of Cervantes's short plays and Calderón de la Barca's philosophical masterpiece, *Life Is a Dream*. Lorca played the role of Sombra, a character who symbolizes death.

During the first six months of 1932 Federico rehearsed the plays that would open La Barraca's tour. He was also busy traveling around Spain, giving a series of talks and doing readings of some of the poems he had written while in New York. He was a famous writer, and wherever he went crowds of fans and enthusiastic audiences filled the theaters to hear him speak.

Back in Madrid, the right-wing press launched an attack on Lorca. The satirical magazine *Gracia y Justicia* called Lorca a *loca*. The conservatives also accused the company of immorality: how could decent young señoritas travel with a group of men?

In the summer of 1932 Lorca completed *Blood Wedding,* the first tragedy in his trilogy of plays about women destroyed by the rigid conventions of Catholic and moralistic Spain. In this play, as in the two tragedies that followed, the deeper theme is sexual frustration. In this drama, as in *Yerma* and *The House of Bernarda Alba,* Lorca may have been projecting his own thwarted love life. It was through tragic heroines—Tennessee Williams's Blanche DuBois is another example—that many homosexual writers of the past expressed their most hidden desires and the frustrations they felt from being considered inferior, tainted beings. Through the women in his plays Lorca can express his own sexual feelings. These women are as marginalized as homosexuals were back then, and they are often persecuted by a dominant machista culture inhospitable to those who dare to challenge the prevailing morality.

Blood Wedding's cry for sexual freedom implies that to deny one's sexual instincts is to die. Leonardo says to the Bride, "To keep still when we're on fire is the worst punishment we can inflict on ourselves." But passion—which liberates—also enchains and dooms in this context. Leonardo says to the Bride, "The moon nails us together. / My loins are fused to your thighs." Passion is the great leveler that drags people to destruction. At the play's end the Bride cries out with anguish, "I was a woman consumed by fire, covered with open sores inside and out, and your son was a little bit of water from whom I hoped for children, land, health! . . . And I would go with your son, who was like a little boy made of cold water, and the other would send hundreds of birds that blocked my way and left frost on the wounds of this poor, wasted woman, a girl caressed by fire! Listen to me! I didn't want to! Your son was what I wanted, and I have not deceived him. But the arm of the other dragged me—like the surge of the sea, like a mule butting me with his head—and would have dragged me always, always, always! Even if I were old and all the sons of your son held me by the hair!"

Like Puig, feminism led Lorca to a rejection of hierarchical thinking—both the patriarchy and matriarchy represented oppression—and to an exploration of the power of sexuality. This naked exploration of the power of the sexual drive is what places Lorca in the company of D. H. Lawrence, Henry Miller, Nabokov, le Marquis de Sade, Anaïs Nin—great liberators of sexuality. With this play Lorca began a relentless attack on the Spanish institutions—church, military, family—that thwarted the liberation of the individual, especially of Spanish women, because Lorca could not at that time have written about homosexuals.

Brazenly, Lorca had begun to make public appearances in which he was accompanied by homosexual young men. For a reading in Barcelona of his New York poetry, Lorca (according to Ian Gibson) was escorted by "an unidentified and somewhat effeminate looking youth with red shoes."

The political situation in Spain was becoming more chaotic. The Anarchist Party, which wanted self-management for workers, opposed both the monarchy and the republic and declared open war on the state. The anarchists wanted a society free from private property, religion, and social classes. The police started to persecute the anarchists, and this led to much bloodshed. The year 1933 began with a massacre by the government's forces of anarchist workers who had rebelled, proclaiming the Libertarian Communist Revolution.

On March 8 *Blood Wedding*, directed by Lorca himself, had its Madrid premiere. The play was a hit with the critics and the public, the former agreeing that Lorca had fulfilled his early promise. Financial success meant that for the first time Federico was independent of his parents. Until this time—with the exception of his trip to the Americas and his years at the Residencia de Estudiantes—Federico had always lived with his parents, which must have made it difficult for him to have lasting, intimate, romantic, and sexual relationships. Lorca belonged to a generation of gay men who lived the life of "the spinster," never marrying and never leaving the family home. Surprisingly, after achieving financial independence, Federico chose to move in with his parents when they rented an apartment in Madrid that spring. In this sense, Lorca was like Jorge Luis Borges and Manuel Puig, who, till the end of their days, lived with their mothers.

With the confidence gained from his smashing success, Federico's political position became clearer and more militant. On May 1 (International Workers' Day), he was the first to sign a petition protesting Hitler's persecution of Jews, gypsies, intellectuals, and homosexuals, among others. Because he was a public figure, Lorca's antifascist politics must have infuriated the Spanish right, which named him one of its declared enemies and made him a target of its intolerance.

By 1933 Federico had a gay circle of friends in Madrid. Eduardo Blanco-Amor, Emilio Prados, and the poets Luis Cernuda and Vicente Aleixandre, all homosexuals, were his frequent companions. At last he was part of a group of predominantly gay men who were not only his contemporaries but also his intellectual and creative peers. Emboldened by his new confidence, Lorca published two acts of *The Public* in a little magazine in Madrid. Because the two acts he allowed the magazine to publish (the first and the fifth) deal with homosexual themes, Federico was finally out as a writer.

During this time Federico met Rafael Rodríguez Rapún, an engineering student who was La Barraca's accountant. Lanky, athletic, masculine, good looking, tormented, Rodríguez Rapún became Lorca's last major love. The student was a womanizer who claimed not to be sexually attracted to men, even if he made an exception with Federico and surrendered to the writer's magnetic personality. It seems safe to say that Rodríguez Rapún was at least bisexual, and it is generally agreed that Rodríguez Rapún is the muse of Lorca's *Sonnets of Dark Love*.

On October 12 Rapún wrote to Federico, who by then was on his way to Buenos Aires, telling him how often he remembered the poet, how hard it was to be apart after having been together constantly for many months. Rapún writes about how attracted he was to Federico and that his consolation was that they would share time together again when Federico returned to Spain. This letter is the only correspondence extant about the love affair of the two men.

By the end of the summer of 1933 Lorca was writing *Yerma,* also based on a real incident and also dealing with a woman's barrenness. In the meantime Lorca's plays had begun to be staged abroad with much success. The production of *Blood Wedding* in Buenos Aires was a triumph. The actress Lola Membrives, who had starred and produced the play in the Argentinean capital, urged Federico to travel to Buenos Aires, but he hesitated. Perhaps Lorca's hesitation was due to the terms of the ungenerous contract or because he was busy touring with La Barraca. It is also likely that he was in love with Rafael Rodríguez Rapún and did not want to be apart from him.

Federico finally made up his mind and booked passage for Argentina. Lola Membrives's Buenos Aires production of *Blood Wedding* ran for several months, and Lorca made a large amount of money. Federico became acquainted with the poet Pablo Neruda. They collaborated on a book called *Paloma por dentro, o sea la mano de vidrio* (Inner dove, that is the hand of glass), with Lorca doing surrealist illustrations of Neruda's poems. The other towering literary figure then living in Buenos Aires was Jorge Luis Borges, who thought Lorca's work exploited the stereotypes of Spanish folklore—bullfights, gypsies, flamenco. After Federico's death Borges used to say Lorca's reputation had been helped immensely by his tragic end.

During his stay in Buenos Aires, Federico met the Mexican writer Salvador Novo (1904–1974), a homosexual and the author of an unpublished memoir that depicts with candor his life as a homosexual in Mexico during the early decades of this century. Lorca became infatuated with Maximino Espasande, a young amateur thespian, a streetcar conductor, and a communist sympathizer. In the predictable version that Espasande's family gives of the liaison, the streetcar conductor did not return Federico's attention.

Federico gave an interview to Narciso Robledal, a local reporter to whom we owe one of the best descriptions of the poet's magnetism: "In front of the mirror, while he shaves the bronzed epidermis, we contemplate his face that looks like a full moon, the very lively, laughing eyes, the generous amplitude of his mouth, the chest of an athlete, his rebellious black hair, as black as a raven's wing. He's a big, gypsy-like boy, full of pride, and of a joy that emanates from his pores with a squandering of vitality."

The Federico of this period is the opposite of the morose, tormented man of New York. He's a celebrity enjoying the perks of fame, a man who has come to terms with who he is.

On April 11 Federico disembarked in Barcelona and went straight to Madrid, where the students of La Barraca eagerly awaited his resumption of his post as director of the company. He had returned to Spain as the fascistic right was ascending. La Barraca itself had come under more attack in the conservative press, and the state was chastised for supporting what was called a troupe of homosexuals. Many newspapers accused the students of perverting the peasants and of being agents of "Jewish Marxism." In Spain at that time the word *Jew* was synonymous with *communist,* and the artists who sympathized with the republic were often labeled as homosexuals.

That summer the famed bullfighter Ignacio Sánchez Mejías came out of retirement. Sánchez Mejías and Federico had been friends for many years. The bullfighter was married but bisexual. One of the most renowned figures of his day, he was admired and courted by many celebrities—Ernest Hemingway among them. The elegy that Lorca wrote on the occasion of the bullfighter's death is one of his most homoerotic poems (Sánchez Mejías was gored on the afternoon of August 11 in the town of La Coruña, and he died of gangrene in Madrid on August 13). The poem, a love song of bereavement, is one of the most famous works in Spanish literature.

Lorca's idealization of Sánchez Mejías verges on the idolatrous. The poem describes the goring of the bullfighter and his wake. *Lament for Ignacio Sánchez Mejías* is divided into four movements. The first contains the refrain "at five in the afternoon." It is at five in the afternoon that a bull wounds the toreador; it is at this "horrifying five in the afternoon!" when "death laid eggs in the wound."

The second movement, "The Spilled Blood," has another refrain: "No,

I refuse to it!" What Federico refuses to see is Ignacio's blood "on the sand." While Ignacio was dying, Lorca could not bring himself to go see his friend. In this section Lorca begins to sing the praises of the bullfighter:

> No prince ever was in Seville
> that could approach him,
> no sword like his sword,
> . . . Like a river of lions
> the marvel of his strength,
> . . . What a great fighter in the ring!
> What a mountaineer on the heights!
> How gentle toward ears of grain!
> . . . How dazzling at the fair!
> How magnificent when he wielded
> the last banderillas of the dark.

Lorca admires Sánchez Mejías for his superhuman strength as well as his tenderness. The bullfighter has the manly attributes of the gypsy heroes of *Gypsy Ballads*. Now that Ignacio has fallen into an unending sleep, his blood "sings through salt marshes and meadows," flowing all the way to the river "Guadalquivir of the stars." Federico refuses to see his hero cut down by death; he wants to remember him in all his magnificence and not deformed by gangrene. In the last verse of this section the poet defiantly exclaims, "I won't look at it, ever!"

Stone is the recurring image in the third movement, stone that "yields no sound, no crystal, no fire— / yields only endless bullrings without walls." In his mind's eye Federico sees "Ignacio the wellborn: lying on stone." What he finds is a horrible image: "Death had overlaid him with pale sulphur / and given him a minotaur's dark head." Ignacio is finished, "Rain seeps through his mouth. . . . The luminous form that once held nightingales / we now see being punctured through and through."

At this point a bereaved Federico asks to be consoled and comforted by "men with harsh voices. / Tamers of horses, subduers of rivers, / whose bones you hear straining, who sing / with mouths full of sunlight and flint." Federico wants these masculine men to show him "a way out" of Ignacio "shackled by death." He wants these men to teach him "to weep like a river." Once again Lorca expresses in these verses an admiration—almost an adoration—of virile, larger-than-life men. Ignacio is as magnificent a creature as Walt Whitman, another godlike creature to be worshipped.

"Absence of the Soul," the final section of the poem, contains the refrain "because your death is forever." This section deals with the world's indifference toward the dead. After Ignacio dies, neither the bull nor the fig trees know him. Only through the poet's grief, and the poetry he writes, does the great toreador continue to live. "Autumn," writes Lorca, "will return bringing snails, / misted-over grapes, and clustered mountains, / but none will wish to gaze in your eyes." Yet Lorca will not be fickle in his affection; he will sing for posterity Ignacio Sánchez Mejías's "profile and grace," and his "gay valor." The poem ends with the moving reminder that "Not soon, if ever, will Andalusia see / so towering a man, so venturesome."

This unabashedly erotic elegy is one of the high points of Lorca's evolution from closet poet ("Ode to Salvador Dalí") to homosexual poet filled with self-hatred (*Ode to Walt Whitman*) to openly gay writer in the *Sonnets of Dark Love,* in which he finally unmasks himself and proclaims his love for another man.

Lorca's final years were a period of febrile creativity: he finished *Yerma* in June 1934. In the fall he completed the comedy *Doña Rosita the Spinster* (about a woman who loves unrequitedly) and the poems of *Diván del Tamarit.* He was also at work on *The Destruction of Sodom,* a play he never finished.

Yerma opened on December 9, 1934. Subtitled *A Tragic Poem, Yerma* is another exploration of the world of women in rural Spain, a distillation of Lorca's feminism. It is Lorca's most articulate statement to date about the condition of Spanish women. Yerma herself is strong-willed woman with powerful sexual drives. She is a forerunner of such Tennessee Williams heroines as Serafina, Alma, Baby Doll, the Princess, Maggie the Cat, and Blanche DuBois. Yerma, married to Juan, is trying to conceive, without success.

The play has two kinds of women: those who have powerful sexual identities and defy convention, and those who have withered in life, defenders of the patriarchy and the status quo. A character named Second Girl says to Yerma, "I'm nineteen years old and I don't like to cook or clean. . . . I have to spend the whole day doing things I don't like! And what for? Why is it necessary for my husband to be my husband? We did the same things when we were engaged that we do now." This woman, who represents the spirit of freedom crushed by conventions, adds, "All the people are stuck in their houses doing things they don't like. You're better off out in the middle of the street! Sometimes I go down to the river, sometimes I climb up and ring the church bells, and sometimes I drink a little anisette." She's the opposite of the conservative women of the town who are comfortable with the old roles and ideas. Commenting on Yerma's barrenness, the Fourth Washerwoman says accusingly, "You have children if you *want* them!" Yet these women have raging sexual drives. The Fourth Washerwoman says, "And our body has / Branches of raging coral."

Although Yerma feels "a wave of fire" sweeping her, her husband has no desire for her. "When he takes me," she says to Dolores, "he is doing his duty, but his body feels as cold as a corpse!" To her husband she pleads, "Don't push me away—want *with* me!" But Juan, who's only interested in keeping up appearances, in looking good in the eyes of society, commands her to be quiet. Yerma replies, "At least let my voice be free."

Yerma's pain is enormous. Marriage, the only place where a woman of that time could succeed, has proved a failure for her. And yet she's full of life, and this is the source of her tragedy: "I'm like a parched field big enough to hold a thousand teams of oxen plowing, and what you give me is a little glass of water from the well!"

In Lorca's view women are the impractical dreamers, whereas men are realists, creatures who have no need for poetry. The play ends abruptly when Yerma murders her husband. For its time *Yerma* was a transgressive, even shocking work.

The premiere of *Yerma* was interrupted briefly to remove provocateurs who taunted the actress and the playwright with cries of "lesbian" and "queer." The play turned out to be Lorca's first smash success in Madrid, although the right-wing press accused the author of immorality.

On the political front the situation was becoming ominous. On May 6, 1935, José María Gil Robles, the new conservative minister of war, named General Francisco Franco his chief of staff. Gil Robles was a fascist sympathizer.

During this period, because of their involvement with La Barraca, Lorca and Rodríguez Rapún were virtually inseparable. Their relationship could not have been entirely satisfactory for Lorca. While Federico had long ago stopped pretending to be attracted to women, Rodríguez Rapún was very much interested in the opposite sex. Ian Gibson reports that one night in Barcelona, "after a binge in a downtown flamenco joint, Rapún had left with a Gypsy girl and failed to return to the hotel where he was staying with Lorca. Federico was in despair, believing that Rapún had abandoned him; and . . . pulled a wad of Rafael's letters out of his pocket to prove the passionate nature of their relationship."

Around this time Federico started writing the *Sonnets of Dark Love.* In the history of homoerotic literature the eleven sonnets that make up the cycle occupy as distinguished a place as Michaelangelo's homosexual poems, the sonnets by Shakespeare that deal with homoerotic content, and the Spanish mystic San Juan de la Cruz's poems of erotic and mystical love.

The sonnets were first published in a clandestine edition of 250 numbered copies in December 1983. Lorca's family was finally pressured to officially publish the eleven sonnets in March 1984 in a Spanish newspaper. Love and death are the themes of the *Sonnets of Dark Love*. Alternately sensual, joyous, sad, tender, anguished, these poems explore the contours of a tempestuous relationship. They are a strip-tease-of-the-soul performance in which Lorca alternately beseeches and implores his beloved. Although Lorca never acknowledged for the record that the poems were inspired by his relationship with Rodríguez Rapún, it is generally agreed that the sonnets were the result of this major but painful relationship. In "Sonnet of the Sweet Complaint," Lorca writes:

> If you are my hidden treasure,
> if you are my cross, my dampened pain,
> if I am a dog, and you alone my master. . . .

Despite the sadomasochistic overtone of these lines, and of the relationship, Rodríguez Rapún gave Lorca a painful requited love that was the source of Lorca's most ecstatic passion. Furthermore, the sonnets are proof that Rodríguez Rapún shared with Federico blissful moments of tenderness and intimacy. A sonnet such as "His Beloved Sleeps on the Breast of the Poet" makes this abundantly clear: "You cannot ever know how much I love you / because you sleep in me, asleep to all. . . . / . . . But sleep, sleep on forever, my beloved."

In *Federico García Lorca y la cultura de la homosexualidad masculina* (Federico García Lorca and the culture of masculine homosexuality), Angel Sahuquillo refers to a letter Lorca wrote in which the poet says that he finds his own poetry pathetic because so far he has been unable to say what he really thinks. But in the *Sonnets of Dark Love* Lorca finally managed to write as a homosexual man with powerful sexual desires. As protracted and tortuous as Federico's journey to express himself as a homosexual had been, by the time he wrote these sonnets, a year before he died, he had accepted his sexuality and come out as a writer. One wonders what other important contributions he might have made to the history of gay literature. But in these eleven sonnets, Lorca, the homosexual poet, emerges triumphant.

As Spain's situation deteriorated, Lorca became more vociferous about his socialist position. To the Madrid newspaper *La Voz* he declared: "The day when hunger is eradicated there is going to be the greatest spiritual explosion the world has ever seen. We'll never be able to imagine the joy that will erupt when the Great Revolution comes. I'm talking like a real socialist, aren't I?"

In April 1936 Luis Cernuda published in Madrid his volume of poems *La realidad y el deseo* (Reality and desire), the first important volume of homosexual poetry published by a Spaniard. Lorca must have been deeply impressed by Cernuda's courage in writing about his sexual inclinations so nakedly; Lorca introduced the book at the party. The two poets had met in 1927; in the 1930s, after Cernuda moved to Madrid, they had become close friends.

In June Lorca finished the last play of his trilogy of tragedies, *La casa de Bernarda Alba,* relating the story of a straight-laced matriarch who thwarts the love lives of her five daughters. The play symbolizes the tyranny and dictatorship Lorca saw on the rise in Spain, where workers, peasants, Jews, emancipated women, and gays had become targets of the fascist forces. I think this play is Lorca's theatrical masterpiece, the work that most nakedly expresses his beliefs. The action opens with the death of Bernarda's second husband. Bernarda orders a long mourning period, warning her daughters that "during our eight years of mourning, no wind from the street will enter this house! Pretend we have sealed up the doors and windows with bricks." She becomes her daughters' jailer, incarcerating them not only physically but spiritually. Bernarda will, however, allow the marriage of Angustias. Because she's the eldest, Angustias has inherited a large dowry, and the other four daughters won't be able to marry until Angustias has wed. She's supposed to marry Pepe el Romano, who is really in love with Adela, the youngest. Everyone knows that Pepe el Romano is going to marry Angustias for her money.

Bernarda's daughters are trapped in her reign of terror, and they are incapable of changing the status quo. Bernarda keeps María Josefa, her eighty-year-old mother, locked up because she is supposedly out of her mind. María Josefa is the only one who dares to express her sexual needs. At one point she says, "No, I won't be quiet! I don't like to see these old maids itching to get married, their hearts turning to dust. . . . Bernarda, I want a man so I can be married and be happy." The mother is a Shakespearean fool who hides behind her madness to tell the truth. What Lorca seems to be saying is that in a house run by a mad person everyone else eventually becomes mad. Bernarda establishes a paranoid society in which she is the only person who is always right. She symbolizes the totalitarian dictators of the twentieth century: Hitler, Mussolini, Stalin, Franco. In this sense the work is prophetic and visionary — after the war all Spaniards had to live for four decades in the house of General Franco.

Bernarda's house is a police state ruled by fear. She sees enemies everywhere. She has her maids spying on the neighbors, and she orders them to chase away the beggars who come to her door asking for alms. Bernarda herself is a kind of Orwellian Big Brother. She says: "I was born with my eyes open. Now I'll keep watch, and never close them until I die." Bernarda's maids are tired of her, the way the Spanish people were tired of the oppression of centuries. These elderly maids represent the Spanish populace, thirsty for justice and revenge. Like the old monarchic state, Bernarda has no compassion. "The poor are like animals," she says, "they seem to be made of other substances."

At the end of the second act the townspeople learn that a young woman has given birth, killed the child, and buried it under stones. The villagers want to kill her. Bernarda, who represents intolerance, asks for revenge. "Kill her! Kill her!" she cries as the curtain drops.

Only two colors mark *The House of Bernarda Alba*. The walls of the house are white. The dresses of the women are black. The house represents Spanish society when all the issues were presented in terms of black and white, a society that had no room for dialogue. Lorca depicts in this play the atmosphere of intolerance that led to the Spanish Civil War. La Poncia, Bernarda's elderly maid, says, "I'd like to cross the ocean and get away from this house at war." The play ends with Adela's suicide. Like her grandmother, Adela is a sexual being: she's unwilling to hide her passion for Pepe el Romano. Nonetheless, right before she dies, she breaks her mother's cane in half. "This is what I do with the tyrant's rod!" she cries out, at that moment liberating herself from her mother and choosing death. Martirio says of her sister's suicide, "She was fortunate a thousand times over—she had him." Martirio speaks for many of Lorca's heroines, who often are willing to face tragedy in order to satisfy their sexual desires. But Bernarda has triumphed. To her daughters she says, "I want no weeping. . . . Did you hear me? Silence, silence, I said! Silence!" With this ending Lorca seems to acknowledge the triumph of totalitarianism over the individual who dares to dream, separate from the blind and conformist masses. Lorca completed *Bernarda Alba* as Spain moved closer to civil war.

Seeking retribution for the death of Lieutenant José Castillo, a left-wing officer of the republic's Assault Guards Police force, the Republicans kidnapped the right-wing leader of the opposition, José Calvo Sotelo, on June 13, 1936, murdered him, and dumped his body by the gates of Madrid's East Cemetery. The slaying unleashed the ire of the conservative forces in Spain, leaving no political middle ground. The army sided with the conservatives. There was no more room for compromise. Now there could be only a civil war.

Fearing for the safety of his parents, Lorca decided he would leave for

Granada to be with them. Violence from the left and the right had been flaring in that city for months. Before leaving Madrid, Federico entrusted the manuscript of *Poet in New York* to his friend José Bergamín, and he gave the manuscript of *The Public,* plus many personal papers, to Rafael Martínez Nadal, instructing him to keep the manuscripts until they met again. In the event that something happened to Lorca, Martínez Nadal was to destroy them. One must assume that the papers contained revealing information about Lorca's private life.

On July 14 Lorca joined his parents in their country house. Three days later Franco announced in a broadcast the creation of a movement of rebels opposed to the Republican government. There was an uprising in the town of Melillas, in Spanish Morocco, and it spread all over Morocco and then crossed the Mediterranean, flaring on the Spanish mainland. Three days later the military officers of the Granada garrison staged a coup, deposing their superiors and taking control of the city. They began daily executions of sympathizers of the republic.

On August 6 a group of Falangists arrived at the Lorca family farm, La Huerta de San Vicente—where Lorca, his parents, and one of his sisters were staying—and searched the premises. Three days later another party of Falangists, looking for an employee of the Lorcases' who was wrongly accused of killing two people, invaded the farm and terrorized the family employees when they couldn't find him. Lorca tried to intervene to stop the violence, but he was attacked physically and called a "little queer."

Finally, Lorca sought sanctuary in Granada at the house of the poet Luis Rosales, a good friend and an admirer. Two of Rosales's brothers were prominent members of the Falange, and Lorca must have felt that his friend would intervene with his brothers to protect him. Lorca remained at this house for a week. In the early hours of August 16 Federico's brother-in-law, Manuel Fernández-Montesinos, the husband of Concha García Lorca, was shot in Granada's cemetery along with a group of prisoners. Later that day Lorca himself was arrested and taken from his hiding place. On August 19, in an olive grove in the village of Viznar, Federico García Lorca, along with a group of prisoners, was shot. According to Ian Gibson, one of Lorca's executioners later boasted that, to finish him off, he had fired "two bullets into his arse for being a queer." Soon after Federico's lover, Rodríguez Rapún, joined the Republican forces and later was killed in battle.

Luis Cernuda's moving elegy about Lorca, "To a Dead Poet (F.G.L.)," reads in part:

> . . . Here spring shines now.
> Look at the radiant young men

101

whom you loved so much when alive,
Ephemeral, passing by together in the brightness
of the sea.
Beautiful naked bodies that
with their exquisite form
Trail desires behind them. . . .

In the lines "Therefore they killed you, because you were / Green in our arid land / And blue in our dark air" (green and blue were euphemisms for homosexuals), the elegy implies that Lorca was murdered as much for his political beliefs as for his uncloseted homosexuality.

The minute the bigots who killed Federico put an end to his earthly life, they gave birth to the myth. As a mythological being, Lorca is one of the most potent figures in literature. They killed Lorca when he was no longer running away from himself as a homosexual, when he had reached his peak as an artist and as a man and had managed to express in a cohesive manner his vision about the destructiveness of patriarchal thinking. How many homosexual writers before him were that lucky? Like Puig, like Arenas, Lorca died in tragic circumstances yet fully realized. And how many of us can claim that much? Decades after his appalling death Lorca still touches us. In *The Curse of the Butterfly,* one of his early plays, a character talks about "a little fresh violet light all aglow." Lorca's light was not little but enormous. He remains a bright, beautiful comet whose scintillating blaze still blinds and dazzles us all.

5

The Other Jaime Manrique
A Dead Soul

I first heard about the other Jaime Manrique in the spring of 1992, shortly after the publication of my novel *Latin Moon in Manhattan*. One night I received a call from a woman who introduced herself as my ex-wife. I told her that I had never been married and that I was a gay man.

"So you are not the Jaime Manrique I'm looking for," she said. She had seen my novel in a bookstore and thought I was her ex-husband. We chatted a bit. She told me that she was a lesbian and she had married Jaime Manrique, who was gay and a Colombian, so he could get his resident visa. After they divorced, she lost track of him.

At that time this didn't seem a remarkable coincidence. In the 1970s, when I was in my early twenties and living in Bogotá, I had met Jaime Manrique Sáenz de Santamaría, a wealthy and aristocratic young architect who was gay and looked like Oscar Wilde. He was a relative of mine, but because of my "illegitimacy" I didn't press our connection. Anyway, I found him snobbish, impossibly Parisian in his outlook. Quite possibly, I was jealous of him. For a moment I wondered whether the man the woman was looking for might be the same person. The last time I had heard about Jaime Manrique Sáenz de Santamaría, he was residing in Paris.

Later in the spring of 1992 I had a book signing at a local bookstore in New York City. After the reading a tall, handsome, patrician-looking man approached me, introduced himself, and told me he had come to the reading because he thought I was the other Jaime Manrique. I asked him as many questions as I could under the circumstances. The other Jaime Manrique was a banker, he explained, and they had worked together for the Mexican National Bank. He was in his early forties (my age at that time). The man added that Jaime was from Santa Marta, where my father and his wife and children had lived. Although I had many questions, I had to turn my attention to the other people at the signing. Later, the way memory hatches what it wants to believe about the past, I embroidered this encounter and thought the man had told me he and Jaime Manrique had been classmates at Harvard. I wanted to believe this; it fit with the story about Jaime Manrique that I wanted to be true.

I became intrigued with my namesake. I told myself that the next time anyone approached me looking for the other Jaime Manrique I'd drill them with questions. I was convinced that this Jaime Manrique and I were more closely related than Jaime Manrique Sáenz de Santamaría. Santa Marta is a small beach resort on Colombia's Caribbean. Manrique is not a common name, so it was unlikely that there was another Manrique family in Santa Marta that was not related to my father's. Perhaps this Jaime Manrique was the son of my father's brother, or the son of one of my half-brothers, all of whom were much older than I.

In October 1992 the metro section of the *New York Times* published an article about Jackson Heights, Queens, that profiled me. It appeared on a Friday, in the middle of the front page of the metro section, with a big picture of me standing on a corner of Roosevelt Avenue. The phone started ringing at 8 A.M. and rang until late that night. One call was from a woman who introduced herself as my cousin. I have maternal cousins living in the States, but I did not recognize her name. She was looking for the other Jaime Manrique. We talked a bit. She said when she saw the photograph in the *Times* she was sure it was her cousin because I looked like him—he had disappeared many years ago, and the family had been trying to locate him ever since. She said, "Our uncle [Jaime's father] is desperate to have news of him." She was disappointed I was not her cousin, but she wished me "continued success" with my endeavors. After she hung up, I realized that I had forgotten to get her name or her phone number.

I didn't hear about Jaime Manrique again until November 1995, when I was living in the Robert Francis House, a little cabin in the woods outside Amherst, Massachusetts.

One rainy Friday afternoon I was awakened from a nap by the phone. The caller was a woman from Cali looking for the other Jaime Manrique. She told me she was in New York to celebrate the thirtieth anniversary of their high school graduation. Back in 1966 a group of classmates had pledged to meet in New York in thirty years. She told me that Jaime's full name was Jaime Manrique Daza, that they had met at Colegio Hispano in Cali where they were graduated from high school.

In the three years that had passed since I had last heard about Jaime Manrique, I had thought about him frequently. This is the scenario I created in my mind: we were cousins, he had come to the States to live openly

104

as a homosexual, had contracted AIDS, did not tell the family for fear of rejection, and had died anonymously in the city. When I mentioned this scenario to friends, they advised me to look up the records in the city morgue. I didn't. What if he hadn't died in New York, after all? I started planning a trip to Colombia, to Santa Marta, to talk to his family, my relatives. In any case, Jaime Manrique grew in my imagination as a mythic creature. In many ways I began to think of him as my double: my relative, my coeval, my gay brother, the one who had grown up with all the advantages of money and social position. The real thing. The one I wished I had been.

In the summer of 1996 I sent out for *The World Book of Manriques,* a publication that turned out to have little useful information about the Manrique name. However, it contains a Manrique International Registry. And there, under the heading of New York State, appeared my name with my address and beneath it was listed a Jaime Manrique living in Flushing, Queens. Could this be the man I had been looking for? I called information to get his number and was informed he was unlisted. I took this to be proof that he was the man who seemed to have fallen off the face of the earth.

Several weeks went by before I finally wrote him a note saying that I was looking specifically for Jaime Manrique Daza. I added that for years people had contacted me, looking for him, and that if he was the same person, and did not want his whereabouts to be known, I'd respect his desire. I included my phone number.

One night in September I arrived home from seeing *A Delicate Balance* on Broadway and found a message from Jaime Manrique Daza. The message said that he was *"muy emocionado"* (very moved) to hear from me. I dreamed about him all night.

That morning, before I called him, I prayed that I'd be respectful of whoever he was. Since I knew he had gone underground, I told myself I'd have to make a special effort to respect his wishes and not frighten him. I called him from work. We had a brief but warm chat. He said he liked many things in my letter, he had stories to tell me that he hoped would please me, he had known of my existence for many years, he had thought about contacting me but hadn't done it because he wasn't sure I desired it. He added that my letter had made his day.

His diction, his accent, reminded me of my father's politeness, his turns of phrase. A part of me mistrusted that comity. Jaime told me I could call him at any hour of the day or night if I wanted to. He added that he wanted to abandon everything at that moment and run to meet me. I replied that in any case I couldn't do it because I was at work. We made a date to see each other the following Sunday.

I feared all the excitement would lead to disappointment. We probably had little in common—he was a banker, I'm a writer. I was sure that because we were gay (and probably related) we could have a nice meeting. Anyway, he did feel like my double on this earth. For the past four years he had taken a kind of mythic importance in my life. I was glad he was not dead.

All day long I fantasized about his looks—I tried to imagine him as unappealing, uncouth, so I could stop the erotic fantasies about the imminent encounter. Whatever it was, it was the end of a chapter that had opened some years back and that now I wanted to close.

I had to work hard not to obsess about Jaime for the next few days. We might be different sorts of men; our differences might be irreconcilable. I could tell I was also important to him—that whatever I'd felt, he had felt to some degree or other and that we'd both fantasized about each other and the moment when we'd meet.

This is a dream I had about Jaime Manrique Daza. I was in a house in Santa Marta with my mother and I was waiting for him to arrive. I had never met him. When he arrived, I was surprised he was heavy—and very nelly. I went up to him to embrace him, and I came up to his chest. He arrived with some friends who quickly evaporated in the dream.

My mother came out to see him and, in an oily manner I hated, said, "Welcome *blanco*" (white man). We were living in a boardinghouse for poor people, most of them black; they did not even seem to speak Spanish. We went into a common area and then a young girl appeared and, to my embarrassment, she tried to sell us refreshments: soda, beer, *jugos* (fruit juices). I commented that we lived in an apartment in another part of the house. Suddenly, Jaime got up and said, "I hate rats! They're trying to come in through the window." I looked at the window and spotted a swarm of bees. We left that room and went into the living room where my mother was sitting at a table having lunch.

As the time of our meeting approached, I hardly slept. The night before we met (the time was yet to be decided), I arrived home and found a message from Jaime. I called him back and we arranged to see each other around three or four. We chatted for a while; an easy intimacy had begun to develop between us. He told me his father was a doctor, that his mother had died two years before. Then he babbled with great animation about this and that, sounding like an affable middle-class woman from Colombia's Atlantic coast. I could tell he was not an intellectual. A friend had warned me that Jaime might not be a fascinating person but that I might still find him enjoyable.

Jaime was two years older than I, but, unlike me, he arrived in the States when he was already an adult, fully entrenched in the Spanish language. He used melodious words such as *esquela*. He sounded sincere and charming—a man of strong emotions. He told me he nearly cried when he got my letter, that he was so moved that he could hardly see what was actually written in my note; he had often thought about calling me; many people had mistaken him for me when they read about me; and he mentioned, specifically, the *New York Times* article. He said that meeting me was a priority, that he felt like a bride meeting her intended.

Something interesting had happened: as the time of our meeting approached, I began to have many sexual fantasies about Jaime. In the dream I had of him in the boardinghouse in Santa Marta, when I'd thrown myself into his arms and he had hugged me, it felt very comforting.

Friends suggested that Jaime and I could become lovers. After talking to him on the phone, I doubted it. He sounded too Colombian, in a way that I find charming but makes me uncomfortable. But I couldn't deny the powerful sexual fantasies I was having about him. When he mentioned—twice—feeling like a bride (he said his best friend had told him he sounded as excited as one), he brought that element into the situation.

When I opened the door of my apartment and saw Jaime Manrique Daza walking toward me, he didn't look like any Manrique I had ever met. He was short, and he didn't have the double chin that runs in my father's side of the family. Jaime Manrique Daza's appearance betrayed the strong influence of his Goajiro Indian roots. I wondered how anyone could have ever mistaken us. On the other hand, being from the Atlantic coast of Colombia, we shared Indian, African, and white blood. In that sense many *costeños* are of a certain generic type—fleshy lips, cinnamon skin, chestnut eyes, dark-brown hair.

We hugged warmly. I still harbored the hope that perhaps we might be distantly related. I decided not to ask any questions, just to let him speak at his ease. This he did. He told me about coming to this country after being graduated from college in Bogotá; he talked about growing up in Cali, where his father was an eminent doctor who had a pavilion named after him in one of Cali's hospitals. This was a mere preamble. What he really wanted to talk about was his mother: she had been a Goajiro Indian princess, a woman of great beauty, descended from one of the great clans of La Goajira peninsula in northern Colombia. I knew that the Daza name is prominent along the Atlantic coast of Colombia, and the Dazas are Goajiro Indians of high rank. He went on at great length about the closeness of his relationship with his mother; his father, Jaime said, had died many years back. Jaime had no siblings. His mother had died two years earlier, and he had gone back to Colombia to be by her side. In minute detail he described her last days and how devastated he was after she died. From his description it seemed her death was the most important event in his life, something from which he would never recover.

I sensed how important it was for him to tell me all this, so although I wanted to question him about our blood connection, I let him express fully the nature of his grief. He was certainly a mama's boy; his mother had been the center of his universe. As he talked about his mother's death, I began to suspect that he was ill with AIDS. There were moments, when the light of the lamp caught his face at certain angles, that I detected the ravages of HIV wasting. Clearly, he had been ill at some point recently, had recovered, and now he looked almost healthy. When he finished speaking about his mother, he talked about his relationship with his lover, a Mexican who had left him for another man a few years before and had moved back to Mexico. Around then he had lost his job as president of the Mexican bank in New York. He boasted nostalgically about what a big shot he was once and how he used to sign checks for millions of dollars and entertain Latin American billionaires. It wasn't clear the circumstances under which he lost his job, but he was bitter about not working anymore. He complained about the impossibility of finding a job in New York after having such an important post.

As the contours of his current life were revealed, it struck me that this was a man whose life had already ended. He talked about his old friends abandoning him after he lost his job and could no longer entertain them lavishly. His mood perked up, his voice warmed, his bitterness relented when he talked about his dog, a blind poodle he loved. Jaime was no longer in touch with any family in Colombia and had no desire to return. I finally brought the subject around to our blood connection. There wasn't one. His father, Dr. Manrique, was from Cali and was doing his internship in Santa Marta when he met Jaime's mother. After Jaime was born, and Dr. Manrique finished his internship, they moved to Cali. Jaime didn't seem to know anything about my relatives in Santa Marta and was not curious about my family.

As he talked, he revealed himself as classist and racist, making many disparaging remarks about poor Colombians and about people of color. He reminded me of so many Colombians I knew who were blatantly prejudiced and lacking in compassion. Although he looked distinctly like a Goajiro Indian, he referred to Colombians as "Indian savages."

I wanted to end our meeting. And yet, at the same time, I started feeling physically attracted to him. In those moments when he didn't look sick with AIDS, he was a good-looking man. He had beautiful hands, a sensual, slender body, his eyes were rich and glossy like the sap of the rubber tree, and his lips were the color of ripe *mamey*. As he described his loneliness, his alienation, how at odds he felt in bars, in the gay community, with other Colombians, I commenced to feel pity for him.

I had many unanswered questions, so I asked him about the woman who called me claiming to be his ex-wife. He denied knowing her. I mentioned the cousin in Long Island who contacted me to say Jaime's father was desperate to find him; Jaime didn't seem to know who she was. When I mentioned the high school friend from Cali who had reached me in Amherst, he was evasive. The only person he seemed to acknowledge was the Colombian banker who had approached me after the book signing. Predictably, Jaime had nothing nice to say about him. In fact, he had nothing benign to say about anyone, except his mother, who was the perfect embodiment of love, kindness, wisdom, and elegance. For the rest of humanity he exuded contempt.

The more I disliked him, the stronger my sexual feelings for him became. I extended my hand, and he took it, and then we got up from our chairs and embraced and kissed and went to my bedroom. We lay in bed, caressing each other. His skin had the heat of the tropics, and there was a softness and tenderness in the way he expressed his desire. As we were undressing each other, I pulled away. I didn't want to cross a line I'd regret later. Jaime seemed disappointed but did not press me.

I invited him to go out to dinner. We went to a Basque place on 14th Street. He seemed disappointed I had not chosen a first-class restaurant. He ordered a steak and ate with a voracious appetite that surprised me. During our meal I tried to tell him that even if he had AIDS he shouldn't feel life was over. I told him about my liaison with an HIV-positive man with whom I had a rewarding relationship. I added that when it ended it wasn't because of the HIV. He received this story with a blank expression. He wasn't interested in anyone trying to offer hope—his misery was all he had left. Because he complained about having nothing to do to fill his hours, I suggested the names of organizations for which he could do volunteer work. A part of me had made up my mind not to see him again, but he talked about how he hoped we would become intimate friends; he even hinted at exploring the sexual attraction.

After we said good-bye that autumn night, I felt cheated and lost on a wintry steppe, a glacial wind howling around me as all my blood slowly bled out of me, my soul escaping my body, leaving me wandering aimlessly in a dark world. An unstoppable sinking feeling of loss and grief grew over the next few days. I've been in close proximity to dying people, but being with Jaime was akin to being with a ghost, a corporeal ghost: he was a man whose heart seemed to have stopped dreaming long ago. His was a dead soul.

A couple of weeks later he called to complain that I had abandoned him. He talked about his loneliness and it was painful to listen to him. It was as if he expected me to fill the void of his life. I said that I was busy, that I would visit him soon. I was busy, but I had no desire to visit him any time soon. We made vague plans to meet in Jackson Heights and to go for a dinner at a Colombian restaurant. He was suffering and I heard in the back of my head Simone Weil's words: "The capacity to give one's attention to a sufferer is a very rare and difficult thing. It is almost a miracle. It is a miracle." It is exceedingly painful to love the unlovable. Yet I felt responsible for having written to him—for having entered his life, making the first move, disturbing his peace.

We made plans to see each other around Christmas. It would be, I told myself, my one Christian act during the season. I would go to him reluctantly after searching for him for many years. But I couldn't bring myself to face him again or come in contact with his affliction.

One morning at the beginning of January, a man called looking for me. He identified himself as Jaime Manrique's Mexican ex-lover. He informed me that Jaime had died the day before, and he had returned from Mexico for the funeral. He was calling because he had found my name on Jaime's night table. He told me where the wake would be on Friday night in Jackson Heights, and he invited me to attend it. Then he broke down crying. He said that Jaime was a complicated person, that he wasn't easy to get along with but that he liked Jaime's defiant spirit and had loved him despite all this.

I asked him the same question I had asked of Manuel Puig's driver-gardener in Mexico: had Jaime died of AIDS? "I don't know," his ex-lover said. "There were things he would not talk about. He was a private person."

I had asked this question not so much out of gossipy curiosity, but because I believed that Jaime, like Manuel Puig, like so many gay Latinos at the end of the twentieth century, had been silenced by fear after a lifetime of rejection.

I debated whether to go to the funeral. I wanted to go so that I could put some closure to this chapter of my life. But I was afraid of confronting Jaime's corpse: after all, like everybody else, I had failed him. I had lured him from his world of shadows and then had shut the door in his face once he had revealed to me his unlovability. This I found unforgivable. So I did not attend his wake, knowing my failure to attend it would haunt me.

Over the next few weeks I spent many hours thinking about the other Jaime Manrique. Not the real person I had met. But the one I had constructed in my imagination: the rich boy who had grown up with all the advantages; the one who, when I was growing up, I would have given everything to be. Rainer Maria Rilke wrote that "perhaps everything terrible is, in its deepest being, something helpless that wants help from us." All the real Jaime Manrique, not the imaginary one, seemed to have wanted from me was help in lightening the burden of his solitude. But I had been unwilling to enter his dark world to bring him comfort. Once he did not fit my image of him, what I wanted to be the truth, I discarded him—carelessly.

Months later I mentioned this story to a friend. He paused to think and said, "Perhaps you met Jaime so you could finally grow up. Perhaps it's time to let go of all that."

I suspect that was the gift the other Jaime Manrique had to offer me.

6

Nowadays

I didn't set out to write this book. Soon after Manuel Puig died, I felt compelled to write down what I remembered about him as a way of clarifying what he had meant to me. In bits and pieces I composed the memoir included in this volume. But two years went by after its completion before I took any steps to get it published. In the meantime Reinaldo had died. Unbeknown to me, *Eminent Maricones* had begun to take shape.

The title is, of course, an allusion, and a kind of homage, to Lytton Strachey's *Eminent Victorians*—a book that affected my evolution as a writer. But I chose the bilingual title because it sums up what I am—a bilingual, bicultural writer—and because of the oxymoronic quality it acquires when these two words stand next to each other. *Maricón* is a word used to connote something pejorative; by implication a maricón is a person not to be taken seriously, an object of derision. Without exception, maricón is used as a way to dismiss a gay man as an incomplete and worthless kind of person.

The three writers who take up most of this book were maricones—homosexual men whose destiny was their sexual orientation. Their lives are a history of the evolution of the homosexual condition in the twentieth century, just as the subjects of Lytton Strachey's book are a compendium of the imperialism of the Victorian age. Now, in retrospect, as this book comes to its conclusion, Puig, Arenas, and Lorca, by virtue of the lives they led, the nature of their achievements, and the substantial contributions they made to altering, and expanding, the consciousness of our culture, seem to me to be just the opposite of what a maricón is to supposed to be and is supposed to do. Puig, Arenas, and Lorca chose to live homosexual lives and to write homosexual works, when to do so was an incredible transgression. By doing what they did, by being true to who they were, they opened the path for all the Latin homosexuals who have followed in their footsteps. And they did it, it now seems clear to me, by standing in defiance of two of the great evils of our century: intransigent Marxism-Leninism and totalitarian fascism. One normally doesn't think of maricones as defining their lives in opposition to forces of this magnitude. Thus Lorca's murder, Arenas's suicide, and Puig's death in exile stand in crystal clear opposition to General Franco's fascistic forty-year regime in Spain, Castro's iron rule of almost four decades in Cuba, and the thousands who were "disappeared" by the Argentinean military in the 1970s. In their works these writers (in addition to being artists of the first rank, supreme innovators) not only spoke for the oppression of the marginal but had the *cojones* that many heterosexual writers lacked. And thus I arrived at the true meaning of *Eminent Maricones*—*locas, patos, jotos*—who achieved true eminence by the courageous audacity of their examples.

I want to make one final connection. The City of New York played an important role in the lives depicted in this volume, including mine. Lorca came to accept himself as a gay man in New York. After his visit to the city he wrote his most original and daring works. It was in New York that Puig escaped from the death threats he received after the publication of *The Buenos Aires Affair,* the first of his novels to deal with homosexuality and politics, his major themes. And it was in New York that he wrote *Kiss of the Spider Woman,* one of the few truly great works dealing explicitly with homosexuality and Marxism. It was also in New York that Reinaldo Arenas wrote, at the end of his life, some of the most beautiful poems by a Latin American author in the twentieth century. And it was here that he dictated, in a rage, an autobiography that is one of the most liberating works ever written and a document that serves as an indictment of what Latin American Stalinist forces, and Fidel Castro, did—not just to homosexuals but to all those who dared to be different, to dissent. Essentially, Lorca, Puig, and Arenas were that—dissenters, not joiners; visionaries, not conformists. They sought not to ally themselves with the status quo. They saw it as a force to be mistrusted because they understood that originality and true daring always inspire a desire to crush, to cage, to destroy.

It seems ironic that men whose lives ended tragically stand, in the end, as victors, as some of the most accomplished citizens of their time. Lorca I met on the page, but Puig and Arenas, whom I was privileged to know intimately, are among the noblest human beings I've ever met. They were unflinching in their beliefs, and their beliefs were tied in with the destiny of those who were oppressed and suffered persecution in their nations. Ultimately, they were engaged writers who defy the definition of what a maricón is supposed to be.

This book also turned out to be an autobiography of sorts. There's much of my life that it's not in these pages, but what there is of it—my intellectual formation, my relationship to a few of my most important mentors, the dark night of the soul I experienced after Manuel and Reinaldo died—is also meant to be read as a triumphant statement. From my earliest childhood to today (I'm in my late forties as I write these pages) my life has been a struggle to find dignity in being a maricón. It is to Lorca and Puig and Arenas that I must give thanks. Their examples have made my path less uncertain. And it is thanks to them, to what they achieved for me, so that I could be free to not censor myself, that I can say that, as I write the last lines of this book, I am a fulfilled human being. I laugh nowadays. Often and with gusto. The world I live in is one of light and not one of darkness, and I want this book, in whatever small ways, to be an inspiration to all the maricones—and heterosexuals—who dream of being men and women capable of taking on whatever kind of windmill stands in their way. Because maricones, as the lives depicted in this book attest, can be the fiercest people.

Source Information

2. MANUEL PUIG: THE WRITER AS DIVA

p. 40 ". . . Guillermo Cabrera Infante wrote that Puig used to say of Carlos Fuentes . . ." "In a Pampas of Dreams," *Review of Contemporary Fiction* (fall 1991).

p. 47 "In an interview he gave me . . ." *El Tiempo* (Bogotá, Colombia), 9 September 1979, p. 3.

4. FEDERICO GARCÍA LORCA AND INTERNALIZED HOMOPHOBIA

p. 74 "In his *Village Voice* article . . . George Chauncey, Jr., writes . . ." George Chauncey, Jr., "The Way We Were: Gay Male Society in the Jazz Age," *Village Voice*, 1 July 1986, pp. 29–30, 34.

p. 74 "Also, the Guatemalan poet Luis Cardoza y Aragón . . . wrote . . ." Ian Gibson, *Federico García Lorca: A Life* (New York: Pantheon, 1989), p. 292.

p. 75 ". . . in *My Last Sigh,* Buñuel's autobiography . . ." Luis Buñuel, *My Last Sigh,* trans. Abigail Israel (New York: Knopf, 1983).

p. 76 "There is a photograph of the pair . . ." Gibson, *Federico García Lorca.*

p. 78 "José María García Carrillo once confided . . ." Gibson, *Federico García Lorca,* pp. 210–11.

p. 80 "Here is Philip Cummings's description of meeting Lorca for the first time . . ." Federico García Lorca, *Songs,* trans. Philip Cummings with the assistance of Federico García Lorca, ed. Daniel Eisenberg (Pittsburgh, Pa.: Duquesne University Press, 1976), p. 23.

p. 81 "In one photograph, taken in Vermont . . ." "Poesía," *Revista ilustrada de información poética* 23–24 (1986).

p. 82 "Dionisio Cañas has written . . ." Dionisio Cañas, "El amigo no identificado de Lorca en América," *El País* (Madrid), 22 December 1985.

p. 84 Luis Cardoza y Aragón has written that one day . . ." Gibson, *Federico García Lorca.*

p. 84 ". . . Barba Jacob was . . . public about his sexual preferences . . ." Leyland

Winston, ed., *Now the Volcano: An Anthology of Latin American Gay Literature* (San Francisco: Gay Sunshine Press, 1979), p. 279.

p. 85   "Lorca called it 'a poem for booing' . . ." Federico García Lorca, *The Public and Play Without a Title,* trans. Carlos Bauer (New York: New Directions, 1983).

pp. 87–88   "Christopher Maurer has called it . . ." Christopher Maurer, "Foreword," in Federico García Lorca, *Once Five Years Pass and Other Dramatic Works,* trans. William Bryant Logan and Angel Gil Orrios (New York: Station Hill Press, 1989).

p. 92   ". . . Lorca (according to Ian Gibson) was escorted by . . ." Gibson, *Federico García Lorca.*

p. 94   Federico gave an interview to Narcisco Robledal . . ." Narcisco Robledal, "El duende se hizo carne" (The Duende Made Flesh), *Federico García Lorca: Conferencias* (Madrid: Alianza Editorial, 1984).

p. 97   "Ian Gibson reports that one night . . ." Gibson, *Federico García Lorca.*

p. 98   "Angel Sahuquillo refers to a letter Lorca wrote . . ." "García Lorca, Federico," in Claude J. Summers, ed., *Gay and Lesbian Literary Heritage: A Reader's Companion to the Writers and Their Works, From Antiquity to the Present* (New York: Holt, 1995), p. 305.

pp. 98–99   "To the Madrid newspaper *La Voz* he declared . . ." Gibson, *Federico García Lorca.*

p. 101   "According to Ian Gibson, one of Lorca's executioners . . ." Gibson, *Federico García Lorca.*

p. 101   "Luis Cernuda's moving elegy about Lorca . . ." Luis Cernuda, *The Young Sailor and Other Poems,* trans. Rick Lipinski (San Francisco: Gay Sunshine Press, 1986).